D1332593

Edexcel GCSE (9-1)
History

Crime and punishment through time, c1000–present

Series Editor: Angela Leonard   Authors: Victoria Payne   Dan Hartley   Trevor Sharkey

PEARSON

Published by Pearson Education Limited, 80 Strand, London, WC2R 0RL.

www.pearsonschoolsandfecolleges.co.uk

Copies of official specifications for all Edexcel qualifications may be found on the website: www.edexcel.com

Text © Pearson Education Limited 2016

Series editor: Angela Leonard
Designed by Colin Tilley Loughrey, Pearson Education Limited
Typeset by Phoenix Photosetting, Chatham, Kent
Original illustrations © Pearson Education Limited
Illustrated by KJA Artists Illustration Agency and Phoenix Photosetting, Chatham, Kent.

Cover design by Colin Tilley Loughrey
Picture research by Ewout Buckens
Cover photo © Science Photo Library / Sheila Terry

The right of Victoria Payne, Dan Hartley and Trevor Sharkey to be identified as authors of this work has been asserted by her in accordance with the Copyright, Designs and Patents Act 1988.

First published 2016

19 18 17
10 9 8 7 6 5 4

British Library Cataloguing in Publication Data
A catalogue record for this book is available from the British Library.
ISBN 978 1 292 12736 1

Printed in the UK by Ashford Colour Press Ltd.

A note from the publisher
In order to ensure that this resource offers high-quality support for the associated Pearson qualification, it has been through a review process by the awarding body. This process confirms that this resource fully covers the teaching and learning content of the specification or part of a specification at which it is aimed. It also confirms that it demonstrates an appropriate balance between the development of subject skills, knowledge and understanding, in addition to preparation for assessment.

Endorsement does not cover any guidance on assessment activities or processes (e.g. practice questions or advice on how to answer assessment questions), included in the resource nor does it prescribe any particular approach to the teaching or delivery of a related course.

While the publishers have made every attempt to ensure that advice on the qualification and its assessment is accurate, the official specification and associated assessment guidance materials are the only authoritative source of information and should always be referred to for definitive guidance.

Pearson examiners have not contributed to any sections in this resource relevant to examination papers for which they have responsibility.

Examiners will not use endorsed resources as a source of material for any assessment set by Pearson.

Endorsement of a resource does not mean that the resource is required to achieve this Pearson qualification, nor does it mean that it is the only suitable material available to support the qualification, and any resource lists produced by the awarding body shall include this and other appropriate resources.

Websites
Pearson Education Limited is not responsible for the content of any external internet sites. It is essential for tutors to preview each website before using it in class so as to ensure that the URL is still accurate, relevant and appropriate. We suggest that tutors bookmark useful websites and consider enabling students to access them through the school/college intranet.

Georgian	Victorian	Edwardian	World Wars	Modern Era

1723
Black Acts make poaching game punishable by death

1735
Witchcraft Act defines witches as confidence tricksters

1831
Last reported case of highway robbery

1833
Tolpuddle martyrs

1837
Victoria crowned queen

1888
Jack the Ripper murders

1916
Military Service Act introduces conscription

1939–45
Second World War

1976
Domestic Violence Act makes domestic violence a crime

1967
Sexual Offences Act decriminalises homosexuality

2006
Racial and Religious Hatred Act makes racial abuse a crime

1700	1800	1900	2000

1685–1815 Enlightenment – new emphasis on science and reason

1748
Fielding brothers set up Bow Street Runners

1777
John Howard's 'The State of Prisons' published

1778
Transportation to Australia begins

1810
Law lists 222 crimes punishable by death

1813 Elizabeth Fry begins visiting prisoners at Newgate

1829
Robert Peel sets up Metropolitan Police

1832
Punishment of Death Act reduces number of crimes punishable by death to 60

1842
Pentonville Prison opens

1857
Transportation abolished

1877 All prisons brought under government authority

1914–18
First World War

1900
Borstals introduced for young offenders

1933
Execution of under-18s ends

1953
Execution of Derek Bentley

1965
Death penalty abolished for most crimes

01 | c1000–c1500: Crime, punishment and law enforcement in medieval England

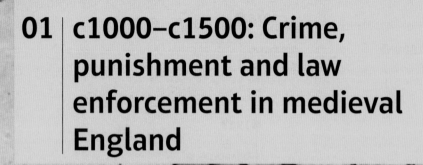

In the year 1000, the people of England and their rulers were Anglo-Saxon. Crime and punishment were dealt with by local communities, with some involvement of the king and the Church.

A dramatic change to everyday life came when the Normans invaded England in 1066. The arrival of the new Norman king, William I, and his nobles, changed England socially, politically and culturally. As they imposed their authority, they redefined some activities that had previously been legal as crimes and they also introduced new punishments and ways of dealing with crime.

The new regime also sparked challenges to government authority.

As the medieval period continued, the growth of towns led to a rise in crime rates in some areas. This stimulated new ideas about law enforcement.

Throughout this period, the Church played an important part in defining and enforcing the law.

Learning outcomes

By the end of this chapter, you will:

- understand how the king, the Church and local communities influenced attitudes to crime and punishment in Anglo-Saxon England
- know about common crimes and typical punishments in Anglo-Saxon England
- know how the law was enforced in village communities
- understand how changes in society, including the Norman Conquest, led to new definitions of crime
- understand the purpose of medieval punishment and why there was continuity throughout this period
- know about the changing methods used to enforce the law
- know how the Church influenced crime and punishment.

1.1 Crime, punishment and law enforcement in Anglo-Saxon England

Learning outcomes

- Know how the king, the Church, and ideas about family, influenced attitudes to crime and punishment in Anglo-Saxon England.
- Know about common crimes and typical punishments in Anglo-Saxon England.
- Understand how the law was enforced in village communities.

Timeline

Crime and punishment in England c1000–c1500

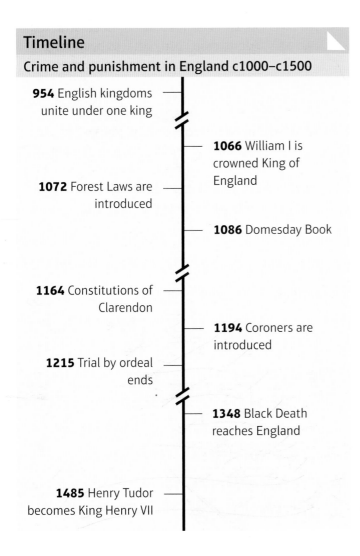

954 English kingdoms unite under one king

1066 William I is crowned King of England

1072 Forest Laws are introduced

1086 Domesday Book

1164 Constitutions of Clarendon

1194 Coroners are introduced

1215 Trial by ordeal ends

1348 Black Death reaches England

1485 Henry Tudor becomes King Henry VII

Picts

Celts

Vikings and Saxons

Figure 1.1 The kingdoms of Britain in c800, before the Norman invasion.

England's population in 1000 was between around 1,700,000 and 2,000,000 and about 90% of people lived in the countryside. Few lived in towns. In rural areas, people lived in small, scattered hamlets and on farmsteads. These communities were very vulnerable to the effects of warfare, bad weather, poor harvests and diseases like the plague. A powerful king and nobility made the law, but village communities and family ties were also strong and helped enforce the law at a local level. The Christian Church was another important influence on ideas about crime and punishment.

During the Anglo-Saxon period there were three important trends in crime and punishment:

- The power and influence of the king over crime and punishment grew. Penalties were increasingly decided by the king rather than local communities.

11

- The role of the Christian Church increased. The Church was concerned with giving those who had committed crimes opportunities to save their souls.
- The use of punishments, including capital punishment, increased. This was intended to help boost the visible power and authority of the king across the land.

The role of Anglo-Saxon kings

King Ethelred II ruled England from 978–1016. During his reign, there was ongoing conflict in the border areas between English and Scottish lands, and some regions were occupied by Viking settlers. In c1000, Ethelred attacked some Viking settlements and also tried to stop Viking attacks by making alliances with Normandy. These actions gave him more control over the kingdom.

Previously, communities had made their own laws, so the crime and punishment system was quite basic and relied on local customs. Now, as the authority of the Anglo-Saxon kings and the territory of England grew, it was increasingly accepted that the king would make and enforce laws. The king relied on advisers to help him govern the country, but he held overall authority, and it was his duty to keep the king's peace*.

Key term

King's peace*

Anglo-Saxons believed that it was the king's duty to take care of law and order, so people could go about their everyday lives knowing that the law would be upheld.

King
Rules the country.
Decides new laws and issues codes of law. Responsible for keeping the king's peace.

Nobles
Given land by the king - wealthy and powerful. Some can advise and persuade the king when making new laws. Appoint shire reeves to make sure people follow the king's law. Responsible for keeping the king's peace in their local area.

Freemen
Rent or own a small piece of land. No say in making the law.

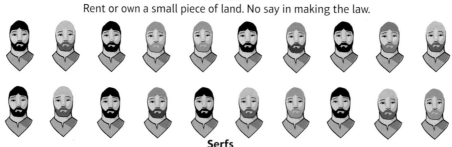

Serfs
Own no land – work for others for very low pay. No say in making the law.

Figure 1.2 The main groups of Anglo-Saxon society.

Across Britain, there was a three-tiered social structure of nobles, freemen and serfs (see Figure 1.2). All three classes were subject to the king's authority. The king ruled in close connection with the noble families. Nobles did well out of this social structure, and they played an important role in keeping it going by backing laws that protected their interests. The king gave nobles land in return for their support.

Actions that threatened this social structure were classed as crimes. These could range from a serf starting a fight with a noble, to what many saw as the worst crime of all – treason*. Crimes of this type are known as 'crimes against authority'.

Crime in Anglo-Saxon communities: towns, villages, abbeys

In c1000, English towns were growing in importance, especially Hamwic (Southampton), Eoforwic (York), and Lundenwic (London). They grew thanks to settled populations, their trade contacts with Europe, and coined money, which made trade much easier. In these larger communities there were more opportunities to commit both crimes against the person* and crimes against property*. There were lots of people in close contact, and it was easier to get away with a crime in a busy town where people did not all know each other well. Also, the concentration of trade goods and money meant that there were plenty of valuable items to steal.

However, most people still lived in villages where everyone knew one another, making it easy to identify and catch a criminal. Local communities were expected to take collective responsibility* for upholding the law; and each area had a reeve* who carried out decisions made by local courts.

Other populations were based around church communities. Several great abbeys* were founded in c1000, as well as many smaller monasteries. In addition to monks and nuns, these communities required daily labourers to run the buildings and supply food and other necessities.

The institution of the Church was very powerful and had particular responsibility for stopping moral crimes* and crimes against the Church. The Church punished those who broke Church laws, for example, by stealing Church property. For more on the Church's role in crime and punishment during the Anglo-Saxon period see page 15.

> ### Key term
>
> **Treason***
> Betraying the king – for example, by helping his enemies, or plotting to kill or replace him.

> ### Key terms
>
> **Crimes against the person***
> Crimes, like assault or murder, that cause physical harm to another person.
>
> **Crimes against property***
> Crimes, like theft, robbery and arson, that involve taking or damaging something that belongs to another person.
>
> **Collective responsibility***
> Being responsible for the actions of other members of your group. In a village community, if somebody broke the law it was up to everyone in the village to take action.
>
> **Reeve***
> A local official, appointed from the community.
>
> **Abbeys***
> Communities of monks or nuns.
>
> **Moral crimes***
> Actions that didn't physically harm anyone, or their property, but didn't match up to society's views on decent behaviour: for example, having sex outside marriage, or not sticking to the rules and customs of the Church.

Source A

Extracts from the *Doom Book*. This was the legal code issued by King Alfred the Great in c893, which was still in force in c1000.

If any one carry off a nun from a minster, without the king's or the bishop's leave, let him pay a hundred and twenty shillings, half to the king, half to the bishop and to the church who owns the nun…

If a man commit folk-leasing [making false accusations that harm somebody's reputation] and it be fixed upon him, with no lighter thing let him make bot [compensation] than that his tongue be cut out…

If any one plot against the king's life, of himself, or by harbouring of exiles, or of his men; let him be liable with his life and in all that he has; or let him prove himself according to his Lord's wer [monetary value of a man's life].

Anglo-Saxon laws

The Anglo-Saxon kings formally issued codes of law. With each new code, new laws could be introduced, existing laws could be altered, and laws that were being ignored could be strengthened.

Activities ?

1 Look at Source A. Write down examples of codes used to stop crimes against:

   a the person

   b property

   c authority

2 What do these laws show about attitudes in society at the time? Make notes under the headings 'position of women', 'use of physical punishments' and 'challenges to authority'.

3 Using information from the last three pages, create a table summarising the influence of kings and the Church on crime and punishment. Use the hints to help you get started.

Anglo-Saxon kings	Anglo-Saxon Church
Create codes of law	Legal position of nuns
Keep the king's peace	Enforce Church laws
…	…

Anglo-Saxon law enforcement

The way that crimes were viewed – in particular, whether they were seen as minor or serious – was based on Anglo-Saxon ideas about justice and how society should be organised. Anglo-Saxons believed:

- the role of the local community in policing the behaviour of others was very important
- that God was the final judge of innocence or guilt
- the status and position of different groups should be clear in law.

The role of the community in enforcing the law

The Anglo-Saxons believed it was a victim's responsibility to seek justice if a crime was committed; but also that the whole community should play a part in delivering justice. Being loyal to your community was seen as a duty.

By the 10th century, English shires were divided into smaller areas called hundreds. Each hundred was divided into ten tithings. All the men (aged over 12) in a tithing were responsible for the behaviour of all the others. One man from each hundred, and one man from each tithing had to meet regularly with the king's shire reeve*. Their role was to prevent crime, particularly cattle theft, in their communities. When chasing a cattle thief a 'hundredsman' was entitled to take two 'tithingmen' with him.

Key term

King's shire reeve*

A man who was appointed locally to bring criminals to justice. The term 'shire reeve' later turned into the word 'sheriff'.

These developments made the community increasingly important in Anglo-Saxon law enforcement.

The whole community was also responsible for tracking down those suspected of crimes. Anyone who witnessed a crime could raise a 'hue and cry' – literally shouting for help. Everyone who heard it was expected to help chase and capture the suspects.

Taking oaths

Anglo-Saxon justice relied heavily on religion when deciding whether someone was guilty or innocent. Oaths* played an important part in proving a person's innocence. Hearings took place in public and the accused could swear their innocence under oath. They could also call upon others in the community to support their claims as 'oath helpers'.

In most cases the accused walked free. This may seem ineffective, but in such small, tight-knit communities it would be very hard for a criminal to get away with a repeat offence. If someone was a repeat offender, or had been caught 'red-handed', then they were not given the option of swearing an oath of innocence.

Key term

Oath*

A formal declaration of the facts, calling on God to witness that what is said is true. A typical oath could start, "I swear before God…"

Trial by ordeal

In cases where there was not enough evidence to prove that a person was guilty, the Anglo-Saxon Church had an important role to play. The accused could be tried by the Church authorities in a 'trial by ordeal'. A trial by ordeal was seen as a way of testing whether the accused was innocent or guilty in the eyes of God. The effect that the ordeal had on the accused was seen as God's judgement on their guilt or innocence.

Trials by ordeal included trials by hot iron, hot water, or cold water. For a trial by hot water or hot iron, heat was used to burn one of the accused's hands, which was then bandaged; if the burn healed well, this was seen as a sign that God judged the person to be innocent. In

a cold water ordeal the accused was thrown into water with their arms tied; anyone who floated was judged guilty, while anyone who sank was judged innocent and hauled up again. This might seem unfair, but to the Church it made sense: an innocent person who sank had been 'accepted' by the water as pure – whereas the guilty had been 'rejected' by it.

Source B

A trial by boiling water, from a medieval manuscript dating from around 1350.

Christian thinking also had an influence on Anglo-Saxon ideas about some punishments. For some crimes including petty theft* the Church advised maiming*. The belief was that, unlike execution, this type of punishment gave the criminal time to seek forgiveness from God.

Key terms

Petty theft*

Stealing small, low-value items.

Maiming*

Causing physical harm. A criminal could be punished by having a hand or ear cut off, or their tongue cut out.

15

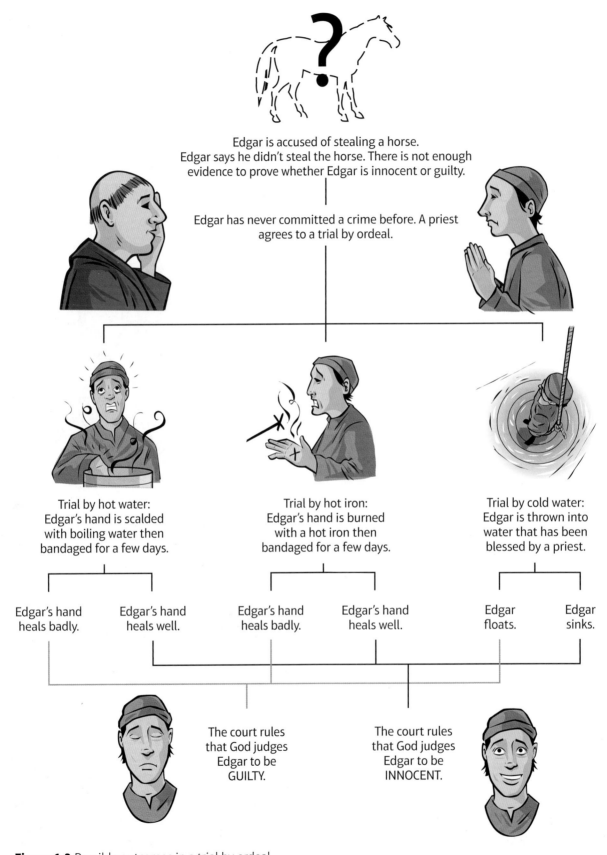

Figure 1.3 Possible outcomes in a trial by ordeal.

Anglo-Saxon punishments

Murder was sometimes punished by fines paid to the victim's family. These were seen as compensation for the loss of life. The fine was called the wergild – which literally translates as 'man price'. The system was intended to reduce blood feuds, in which members of the victim's family killed the murderer, whose family then killed his murderers, and so on – creating an ongoing cycle of violence.

Wergild was paid directly to a victim's family. The fines payable were decided by social status. As the table below shows, your class affected how much your life was judged to be worth.

Rank	Wergild
Prince	1500 shillings
Yeoman farmer	100 shillings
Serf	40 shillings

Capital and corporal punishment

Some crimes received capital* or corporal punishment*. These were a form of retribution*, but were also used as a deterrent*.

Key terms

Capital punishment*
The death penalty.

Corporal punishment*
A range of punishments that caused harm or pain to the body – including being beaten or having body parts removed.

Retribution*
A severe punishment, meant to match the severity of the crime.

Deterrent*
A punishment that is frightening or painful, and designed to put other people off committing the same crime.

Treason and arson (which was viewed as very serious as it damaged the land and property of the ruling classes) were punished by execution – usually by hanging.

For lesser crimes, corporal punishments, including mutilation, could be used. Corporal punishment was meant to act as a deterrent, to help stop other people from committing similar crimes. Punishments like eye-gouging, or removing a hand or foot, sound very harsh, but they were seen as a more lenient alternative to the death penalty. Also, criminals who survived these disfiguring punishments served an important function by reminding others of the consequence of committing crimes.

Source C

Skeletons found during an archaeological excavation at Walkington Wold in East Yorkshire. Archaeologists discovered 12 skeletons in total, all belonging to adults, and all missing their skulls. The skulls were later found buried nearby and had no jawbones. The archaeologists speculated that they had rotted away while the heads had been on public display. Although the bodies were found close together, they had been buried on separate occasions. The archaeologists concluded that they had uncovered an Anglo-Saxon execution cemetery.

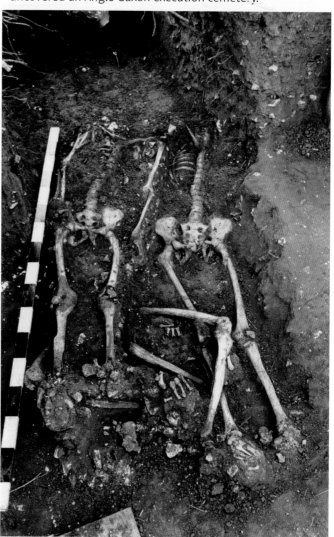

The stocks and the pillory

Public punishments, using the stocks or pillory, were a combination of physical pain and discomfort and public humiliation. The pillory secured the arms and neck (the Anglo-Saxons called the pillory a 'catchneck'). Stocks secured the ankles. The stocks or pillory were placed outdoors, usually at the centre of a town or village, in full view of the neighbours. Those receiving the penalty would be exposed to bad weather, sometimes for several days. The public might also add to their humiliation by throwing rubbish or verbally abusing them.

Crime		Punishment	
Crimes against the person	Murder Assault Public disorder	Wergild Maiming Stocks or pillory	
Crimes against property	Theft Counterfeiting coins Arson	Fines or maiming Hand chopped off Hanging	
Crimes against authority	Treason Betraying your lord	Hanging	

Figure 1.4 A summary of Anglo-Saxon crimes and punishments.

Summary

- Anglo-Saxon kings ruled the unified kingdom of England. They wrote codes of law and enforced those laws.
- The king was supported by nobles who maintained the crime and punishment system.
- Anglo-Saxon society aimed to keep the peace through community law enforcement.
- Physical punishments and maiming were used as a deterrent.
- The wergild system of fines was introduced as an alternative to blood feuds.
- Some serious crimes were punished by the death penalty.
- The Church was also powerful. It was responsible for trials by ordeal.

Checkpoint

Strengthen

S1 What does 'wergild' mean?

S2 Describe two ways the community took part in enforcing the law.

S3 Give an example of an Anglo-Saxon punishment that varied according to the social standing of the victim.

Challenge

C1 What part did nobles play in enforcing the law?

C2 Explain what happened in a trial by ordeal.

C3 Choose two punishments from this chapter and for each explain in what ways it was a deterrent, and in what ways it was retribution.

How confident do you feel about your answers to these questions? Form a small group, discuss the answers, then rewrite improved answers in your group.

1.2 Crime, punishment and law enforcement in Norman England

Learning outcomes

- Understand how the Norman kings increased their authority.
- Know about new laws introduced by the Normans, including the Forest Laws.
- Know about new punishments introduced by the Normans, including the Murdrum fine and trial by combat.

1066, the year of the Battle of Hastings, is one of the most famous dates in British history. Before this time, England's crime and punishment code was quite unified, and Anglo-Saxon kings, nobles and the Church all had important roles in ensuring law and order. After the Norman conquest of 1066, when William the Conqueror took the throne, the power of both the king and the Church increased relative to other parts of society.

Norman rule in England

William of Normandy (later known as William the Conqueror) said he had been promised the English throne by the old king, Edward the Confessor; but there

Figure 1.5 The main factors influencing changing definitions of crimes and how crimes were punished during the Norman period.

An image from the Bayeux Tapestry, showing Norman soldiers setting fire to a Saxon house.

were other claims to the throne and William had to take it by force. William's reign marked an important change in crime and punishment. During the Norman period, the influence of the king over the law increased. Punishment and law enforcement became more centralised and fewer decisions were taken by local communities. William's reign also saw an increased use of harsh punishments, including execution, which were intended to help boost the visible power and authority of the king across the newly conquered land.

The increased powers of Norman kings

Rebellions and the Norman response

Between 1066 and 1087, William I took control of England. He was determined to establish his royal authority and a stronger and more centralised approach to crime and punishment. There was resistance from the Anglo-Saxons, including rebellions in York and East Anglia, and William used brutal means to force the people to submit and to unite England under his control. His decisions about how to deal with the rebellions show that his power as king was without limits. He could order extreme punishments for the rebels, and also punished large groups of people who were not directly involved, to show his power. For example, farmlands were destroyed and animals were

An extract from the Historia Ecclesiastica (Church History) by a priest called Orderic Vitalis, written between 1109 and 1141 to chronicle the history of England through that period.

In his anger he commanded that all crops and herds, chattels and food of every kind be brought together and burned to ashes with consuming fire... As a consequence... so terrible a famine fell upon the humble and defenceless people, that more than 100,000 Christian folk of both sexes, young and old alike, perished of hunger.

killed. Some estimates suggest that 100,000 people died of starvation as a result of food shortages caused by the punishments that William ordered.

Activities ?

1 What does Source B suggest about William's role in law and order?

2 In what ways were William's powers greater than those of Anglo-Saxon kings in maintaining law and order and establishing royal authority?

Norman castles

William and his supporters started a massive programme of castle building. Norman castles were placed in every part of the kingdom. Peasant* workers were made to build the castles in which Norman lords would live, and

Key term

Peasant*

A poor person living in the countryside, who owns little or no land and works for others.

from where they would control the local population under Norman law. The castles were designed to keep a careful watch on communities and to look intimidating – reminding those who lived outside of their place in society. Castles represented the increasingly strong royal authority over law and order in England.

Source C

Dover Castle, one of the best-preserved Norman castles.

The feudal system

Norman society was organised around the feudal system – see Figure 1.6.

King
Owns all the land in the country.
Makes laws. Gives some land to nobles.

Nobles
Given land by the king – wealthy and powerful. Some have castles to help them control their area and enforce the law. In return supply the king with soldiers and horses for the army. Give some land to knights.

Knights
Live on a smaller area of land. Fight for nobles and the king.

Serfs
Own no land – work for nobles or knights for very low pay. No say in making the law.

Figure 1.6 The feudal system in Norman England.

21

In the feudal system, everybody owed money or service to the class above them. Only the king was free to do as he wanted. Under this system, the Normans replaced the Anglo-Saxon nobles with those of Norman descent.

Anglo-Saxon serfs were legally bound to work for their lord and were not allowed to leave their village. Running away was a crime – if anyone tried, they would be hunted down and severely punished.

Interpretation 1

From *Inside The Medieval Mind*, a documentary presented by Professor Robert Bartlett in 2015.

Inequality and oppression were part of the natural order ordained by God. This was a class system of staggering extremes and every class had an exact price. Just like an animal, a human life could be measured exactly.

Murdrum – a new law

The Normans used the law to establish control over the Anglo-Saxon population. If a Norman was murdered by an Anglo-Saxon, and the murderer was not captured and executed, there was a special penalty known as the murdrum fine. This was a large sum of money paid by the hundred where the body was found. This was supposed to stop the increase in revenge murders that took place after the Norman invasion, and make it less likely that people would cover up the crime of a neighbour.

Although the Normans created this new law to protect their authority, the murdrum fine also shows continuity with the Anglo-Saxon system of shared responsibility for the behaviour of everyone in a tithing (see page 14)

Activities ?

1   Write a paragraph explaining how the murdrum fine was used. Use Interpretation 1 and Source D.

2   There are similarities and differences between the murdrum fine and wergild. Make a list of similarities and differences.

3   Now compare your list with a partner's. What did you agree on? What alternative points has your partner made? Write a short paragraph summarising all the points you have made between you.

and with the Anglo-Saxon idea of making a financial payment as compensation for loss of life.

Source D

The murdrum law, enacted by William I in 1070.

[If a Norman is killed] his murderer's lord shall capture the slayer within 5 days if he can; but if not, he shall start to pay me forty-six marks of silver... But when they are exhausted, the whole hundred in which the slaying occurred shall pay in common what remains.

William I's Forest Laws

William declared large stretches of the English countryside to be 'royal forests', which he would use for hunting. After a visit to Hampshire, William took control of what he called the 'Nova Foresta' (New Forest). Around 40 village communities were evicted from the forest in order to clear the new 'royal playground' for hunting.

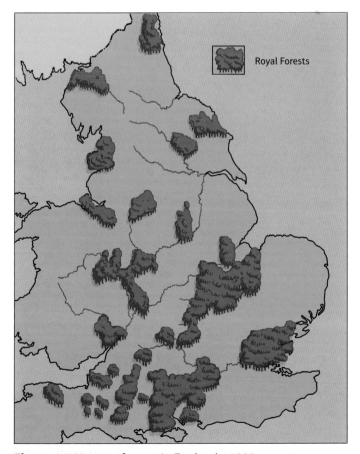

Royal Forests

Figure 1.7 Norman forests in England, c1200.

Source E

An illustration of a medieval hunting scene.

The Forest Laws meant that what had previously been common land – where peasants had the right to graze animals, take firewood, or catch a few rabbits – was now strictly controlled by the king. Only those who could afford to pay for hunting rights would now be allowed to hunt there. For peasants, it became illegal to carry hunting weapons or even take a fallen branch. Hunting wild animals for food was now treated as a crime called poaching*.

The Forest Laws led to much bitterness, as they took away people's access to natural resources, and took away what they saw as fundamental freedoms. Ordinary people saw the Forest Laws as unjust and unfair and, therefore, did not frown upon those who broke these laws.

The Forest Laws created what are known as 'social crimes' – actions that are technically against the law but which most people in society do not disapprove of.

The king hired men to work as foresters to enforce the Forest Laws, and catch poachers and anyone else who did not have permission to come into the forest. Anyone who was caught faced punishments, including hanging and corporal punishments such as castration and blinding. The punishments were deliberately harsh and intended to deter others from poaching.

Key term

Poaching*

Illegal hunting on land that belongs to someone else.

Source F

From the chronicles of Abbot Adam of Eynsham, written in the early 13th century.

The worst abuse in the kingdom of England was the tyranny of the foresters... For them violence took the place of law, extortion was praiseworthy, justice was an abomination and innocence a crime...

Activities ?

1 Choose two words or phrases from Source F that describe the behaviour of foresters, and explain what they mean. Look them up if you need to.

2 Why were the Forest Laws so resented by peasants? Give three reasons.

3 Why do you think William wanted to stop poachers?

Outlaws and the forest

Starting in the Anglo-Saxon period, any man, aged 14 or over, who tried to avoid trial and punishment by running away from his community, was declared an outlaw. Women who ran away were said to be 'waived'. Outlaws and waived women lost the protection of the law. They could be killed without any legal consequences for the person responsible.

Outlaws have strong links with the forest. The Robin Hood story, which first appears in written literature in the late 14th century, is set in the forests of Norman England. Robin and his outlaw gang are described as brave and heroic as they challenge the injustice of the Norman authorities.

In reality, outlaw gangs were very different to Robin Hood and his 'merry men'. For example, the Folville gang was a group of up to 50 outlaws, who operated in England in the 14th century. They carried out many serious crimes, including kidnaps, robberies, rapes, attacks and extortion of money, over a 20-year period. The gang's leader was Eustace Folville, whose father was a lord of the manor in the Midlands. It is likely that his wealthy and influential friends helped the gang avoid capture.

Source G

Woodcut of Robin Hood from the 16th century.

Exam-style question, Section B

Explain why the Normans made changes to crimes and punishments after the Norman Conquest.

You may use the following in your answer:

- the Forest Laws
- the murdrum fine.

You **must** also use information of your own. **12 marks**

Exam tip

The question tests your knowledge and your understanding of causation. You need to focus on factors that help explain why the Normans made changes to the definition of crimes and to punishments. You could use the examples given in the prompts to get you started, but don't forget to include plenty of your own ideas and specific points.

Between c1500 and c1700, attitudes towards many crimes were similar to those held in the Middle Ages. However, the changing religious situation in England led to many religious beliefs and activities being newly classed as crimes.

Religious change and changing definitions of crime

In the 16th century, Europe was rocked by religious instability and conflict. In 1517, a German priest called Martin Luther protested against what he saw as corruption in the Catholic Church. Luther's followers (like others who wanted church reform) became known as Protestants. Protestantism grew as more people came to believe the Catholic Church needed reform – this movement is known as the Reformation.

While some people, including Edward VI and Elizabeth I, followed Protestantism, others stayed committed to the Catholic Church. It was very important to these rulers that their subjects followed their religious lead.

The many changes to the law during this period show just how much power the monarch had in deciding what counted as criminal activity, and how the definition of a crime could change rapidly depending on the views of the person on the throne at the time. A change of ruler could make the everyday religious activities of Protestants or Catholics into criminal acts.

Heresy and treason

The two most serious crimes connected with the religious changes were heresy and treason.

Heresy was seen as a crime against the Church and an offence to God. Heretics (people who committed heresy) were seen as a danger to others – as they could persuade others to follow them in false beliefs.

Treason was a challenge to the authority of the ruler. It became connected with heresy in this period because all monarchs from Henry VIII onwards (except for Mary I) were head of the Church of England. Anyone who challenged the ruler's authority as head of the Church of England would be guilty of treason.

Henry VIII
Ruled – 1509–47
Religion – Catholic

Religious changes
In 1534, following arguments with the Catholic Church about his marriage and divorce, Henry declared himself head of the Church of England. Henry remained a Catholic to the end of his life but closed down Catholic monasteries and seized their wealth and land.

Crimes and religion
Both Protestants and Catholics were punished as criminals during Henry's reign. Protestants were executed for heresy. Catholics were executed for treason as they would not take the Oath of Supremacy, acknowledging Henry as head of the Church of England.

Edward VI
Ruled – 1547–53
Religion – Protestant

Religious changes
Edward was brought up as a Protestant. When he became king he introduced a prayer book written in English, allowed priests to marry and made church interiors plainer – all these actions are typically Protestant.

Crimes and religion
Some Catholic bishops were imprisoned in the Tower of London. Two people were executed for crimes of heresy.

Mary I
Ruled – 1553–58
Religion – Catholic

Religious changes
Like her husband, the Spanish king Philip II, Mary was a strict Catholic. She tried to restore the Catholic church in England and made the Pope head of the English Church once more.

Crimes and religion
Almost 300 people were executed as heretics for refusing to follow the Catholic faith during Mary's reign.

Figure 2.1a Religious change and changing definitions of crime in England, 1509–1625.

Burning at the stake – the punishment for heresy

Heretics were punished by being 'burned at the stake'. The person being executed was tied to a wooden post, or stake, while a fire was lit beneath them. Death was caused by breathing in fumes from the fire, or by the shock to the body caused by the burns.

Executions for heresy during the Tudor period

Monarch	Reign	Executions for heresy
Henry VIII	1509–47	81
Edward VI	1547–53	2
Mary I	1553–58	283
Elizabeth I	1558–1603	5

Source A

An illustration from the *Book of Martyrs*, a Protestant book about people killed for their religion, published in 1563. Three women and an unborn child are being burned at the stake.

42

Elizabeth I
Ruled – 1558–1603
Religion – Protestant

Religious changes
Elizabeth tried to find a 'middle way' in religion. She wanted to create a Protestant Church that was not too challenging to Catholic traditions, so English Catholics would feel comfortable as part of the Church of England, with her as its head.

Crimes and religion
In 1559 Elizabeth passed several new laws about religion:

• The Act of Uniformity said everyone had to go to church on Sundays and holy days or pay a fine. Those who refused were labelled 'recusants'. At first they were only prosecuted after refusing to attend church several times.
• The Act of Supremacy reintroduced the Oath of Supremacy. Catholics who refused to swear it were committing a crime.
• The harsh heresy laws introduced by Mary I were repealed.
In 1569 there was a Catholic rebellion in the north of England and in 1570 the Pope excommunicated* Elizabeth. After this many more Catholics were prosecuted for recusancy, and hundreds of rebels were executed.

James I
Ruled – 1603–25
Religion – Protestant

Religious changes
James was Protestant but was tolerant towards Catholics at first. However, the Gunpowder Plot in 1605 changed his attitude.

Crimes and religion
James introduced strict anti-Catholic laws. The 1605 Popish Recusants Act forced Catholics to swear loyalty to the King and pay heavy fines for not attending church.

Figure 2.1b Religious change and changing definitions of crime in England, 1509–1625.

Key term

Excommunicate*

Eject from the Catholic Church. By excommunicating Elizabeth I, the Pope was saying she was no longer a member of the Church.

Not everybody accused of heresy was burned at the stake. Most people took the opportunity to recant*. They were made to take part in a public display that involved carrying wooden sticks to the place where their burning would have taken place. The sticks were then burnt symbolically.

Key term

Recant*

Make a public statement that you have changed your religious beliefs.

Extend your knowledge

Fox's *Book of Martyrs* and Bloody Mary

The *Book of Martyrs*, by John Fox, was published in 1563, and described persecution of Protestants by the Catholic Church and English Catholic monarchs, including Mary I. The book calls her 'Bloody Mary' because of the large numbers of people killed during her brief five-year reign. In addition to the executions, more than 800 Protestant clergy were forced to flee abroad. Mary was married to the Catholic King of Spain and was influenced by Spanish attitudes to heresy. In Spain, heretics were investigated by the much-feared Spanish Inquisition, which punished Protestants using torture.

Activities ?

1 Explain briefly why holding religious beliefs that were different to the monarch's was treated as such a serious crime.

2 Why were heretics executed by being burnt at the stake?

3 Using information from Figure 2.2 and the table showing executions for heresy in the Tudor period, create two spider diagrams to explain Henry VIII's and Mary I's attitudes and actions towards heresy. Write a short paragraph comparing the two monarchs.

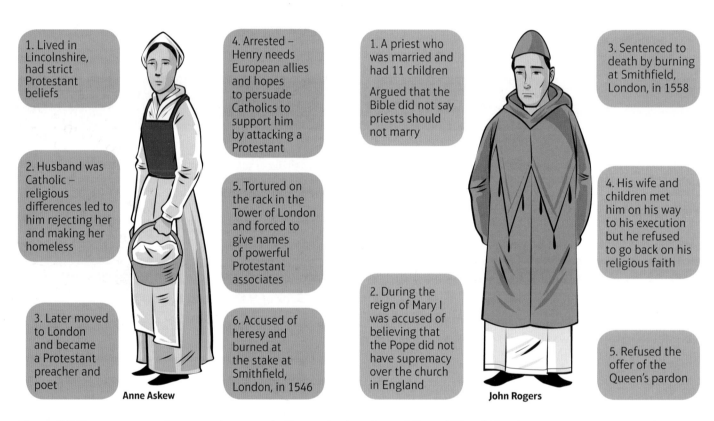

1. Lived in Lincolnshire, had strict Protestant beliefs

2. Husband was Catholic – religious differences led to him rejecting her and making her homeless

3. Later moved to London and became a Protestant preacher and poet

Anne Askew

4. Arrested – Henry needs European allies and hopes to persuade Catholics to support him by attacking a Protestant

5. Tortured on the rack in the Tower of London and forced to give names of powerful Protestant associates

6. Accused of heresy and burned at the stake at Smithfield, London, in 1546

1. A priest who was married and had 11 children

Argued that the Bible did not say priests should not marry

2. During the reign of Mary I was accused of believing that the Pope did not have supremacy over the church in England

John Rogers

3. Sentenced to death by burning at Smithfield, London, in 1558

4. His wife and children met him on his way to his execution but he refused to go back on his religious faith

5. Refused the offer of the Queen's pardon

Figure 2.2 The treatment of two people accused of heresy in the reigns of Henry VIII and Mary I.

2.3 Case study: The crimes and punishment of the Gunpowder plotters, 1605

Learning outcomes

- Know why the Gunpowder plotters decided to act against the Crown.
- Understand what crimes the plotters were accused of.
- Understand why they were punished so harshly.

Timeline
The Gunpowder Plot

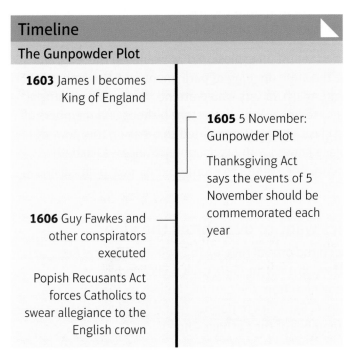

1603 James I becomes King of England

1605 5 November: Gunpowder Plot

Thanksgiving Act says the events of 5 November should be commemorated each year

1606 Guy Fawkes and other conspirators executed

Popish Recusants Act forces Catholics to swear allegiance to the English crown

Source A shows the gruesome execution of Guy Fawkes – the most famous of the Gunpowder plotters – who was hanged, drawn and quartered in 1606. This type of execution was only used for those found guilty of committing the most serious crime – treason. Guy Fawkes and his fellow conspirators* had plotted to kill the king and therefore received the most severe punishment possible.

Key term

Conspirator*

Someone who is involved in a conspiracy – a secret plan to do something illegal.

Elizabeth I died in 1603, after reigning over England for 45 years. Catholics across the country were hopeful that the new king, James I, who was married to a Catholic, would allow them more religious freedom. However, over time, it became clear that James was prepared to introduce stricter anti-Catholic measures and so Catholics were disappointed.

As Protestant rulers, both Elizabeth and James were very wary of Catholic plots against the crown. Elizabeth even had her own cousin, Mary Queen of Scots, executed in 1587, when she suspected she was involved in an assassination plot.

Source A

An engraving showing the execution of Guy Fawkes and his fellow conspirators, produced in 1606.

Activities

1. Look at Source A and think about what those who were present at the execution could see, hear, smell and feel. Describe the scene.
2. What was the intended impact of this method of execution on onlookers and the general public?

The goals of the Gunpowder plotters

Guy Fawkes is the best-known of the gunpowder conspirators, but he was not the leading figure. That was Robert Catesby, who had a history of Catholic resistance. His father had been imprisoned for hiding a Catholic priest, and he had refused to take a Protestant oath, which meant he could not finish his university degree. He was responsible for recruiting the other Gunpowder plotters, including: Guy Fawkes, Thomas Percy (a royal bodyguard), Thomas Winton (Catesby's cousin) and Jack Wright. Some historians claim that the group viewed themselves as religious soldiers, who saw it as their duty to attack the English state.

The conspiracy aimed to set off an explosion that would kill the king, and those close to him, at the state opening of parliament on 5 November 1605. The elite of Protestant English society would attend this important official occasion. They included senior judges, Protestant bishops and members of the aristocratic ruling class. The plotters wanted to break up this powerful ruling group and replace James I with his daughter, Princess Elizabeth, who they would influence and control to promote their own political and religious aims.

Why did Catholics want to overthrow the king?

Protestantism had been the official religion in England since the Act of Uniformity was passed in 1559. In 1570, Queen Elizabeth I was excommunicated (disowned) from the Catholic Church by the Pope. The Pope called upon all loyal Catholics to depose (get rid of) Elizabeth because she was no longer a member of the Catholic Church.

Following Elizabeth's excommunication, Catholics in England were more actively prevented from practising their faith, and were punished if they continued to do so. Catholics were not allowed to hear mass, or be married or baptised by a Catholic priest. Attending the local, Protestant, parish church was compulsory, and Catholics who refused to go were treated as criminals and fined.

The plan

The conspirators first met on 20 May 1604, to begin organising the attack. They rented a house in central Westminster next to the parliament buildings. Guy Fawkes pretended to be a servant who was looking after the house while his employer was away. They then rented a cellar directly under the House of Lords and packed it with an estimated 36 barrels, holding at least one ton of gunpowder in total.

Activities ?

1 Make a list of reasons Catholics had to overthrow King James I. Rate each reason with a score from 1–10, with 1 being a minor reason and 10 a very strong reason.

2 Compare your scores with a friend and explain your reasons.

3 Write a short paragraph explaining why the Gunpowder plotters wanted to overthrow James I.

Source B

The members of the Gunpowder Plot in a 17th-century engraving.

The plot fails

On 20 October 1605, Lord Monteagle received a letter warning him not to attend the ceremonial opening of parliament. Monteagle gave the information to Robert Cecil, the king's spy master, who ordered that Westminster should be searched. It was in this raid that the gunpowder and Guy Fawkes were discovered.

Some historians argue that the authorities knew all about the plot in advance, but let it proceed so that Catholic rebellion would be brought into the open, and there would be clear justification for further Catholic persecution. During preparations for the attack Fawkes had travelled to Flanders to look for foreign assistance. His actions were monitored by English spies who informed Robert Cecil of what Fawkes was doing.

Questioning, trial and punishment

Torture was only legal in England if the king gave specific orders to use it in exceptional circumstances. Guy Fawkes and his fellow conspirators were tortured to extract confessions about their role in the plot. The most feared method of torture was known as the rack: a wooden frame that was used to stretch the body, forcing limbs apart at the joints. Guy Fawkes was questioned using this method of torture at the Tower of London as part of the investigation into the plot. At first he refused to confess, or give up the names of his co-conspirators; but on 17 November, 12 days after his arrest, he finally confessed.

Source C

An order sent by James I to the Tower of London on 6 November 1605, giving his permission to torture Guy Fawkes in order to extract his confession and persuade him to name his accomplices.

If he will not other wayes confesse, the gentler tortours are to be the first usid unto him... God speed youre goode worke. James.

Source D

Extract from Guy Fawkes' confession:

Catesby suggested... making a mine under the upper house of Parliament... because religion had been unjustly suppressed there... twenty barrels of gunpowder were moved to the cellar... It was agreed to seize Lady Elizabeth, the king's eldest daughter... and to proclaim her Queen.

Source E

Documents featuring Guy Fawkes's signatures before and after torture.

Activities ?

1. In groups, use the text and Sources A–D to create a storyboard showing the actions of the plotters and the response of the authorities. Remember their priority was deterrence – to reduce the threat of further attacks.

2. Compare your work with another group and discuss any differences in your approach.

After their capture, the conspirators' trial began in January 1606, and they were found guilty of treason. They were sentenced to death by being hanged, drawn and quartered. This meant that they were hanged then revived, had their genitals cut off and burnt, and were then disembowelled; finally, their limbs and heads were chopped off. The authorities were determined to make the punishment a deterrent to others who might want to plan a similar attack. At this time of religious instability, they were concerned that other Catholics might want to plot against the king. This extreme public punishment was viewed as the appropriate penalty for this type of crime.

Longer-term consequences of the plot

The 'King's book' published soon after the uncovering of the plot, included an account by James himself of the events of the plot, alongside Fawkes' confession. This helped encourage anti-Catholic attitudes.

In 1605, the Thanksgiving Act ordered that the events of 5 November should be commemorated each year, and Catholics were banned from working in the legal profession or becoming officers in the armed forces.

In 1606, a law called the Popish Recusants Act forced Catholics to take an oath of allegiance to the English crown. They were also forced to take part in Church of England services and rituals – or pay fines.

The plot continued to have an impact on Catholics in England for centuries after the event. They were restricted from voting, becoming MPs, or owning land. They were also banned from voting in any elections until 1829.

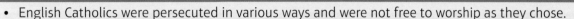

Summary

- English Catholics were persecuted in various ways and were not free to worship as they chose.
- The Gunpowder Plot, led by Robert Catesby, aimed to blow up the king and those close to him at the state opening of parliament in 1605.
- The plot was uncovered and the conspirators were found guilty of treason. They were sentenced to death by being hanged, drawn and quartered.
- Following the plot, Catholics experienced more persecution, and were excluded by law from voting and becoming MPs for many years.

Checkpoint

Strengthen

S1 Summarise the main complaints of English Catholics during the reign of Elizabeth I and James I.

S2 Why were Catholics hopeful that James I would introduce greater religious freedoms?

S3 List the main Acts of Parliament mentioned in this section and briefly explain what the new laws involved.

Challenge

C1 Why did it suit the Protestant authorities to uncover such a serious Catholic-led plot?

C2 Why was such a gruesome method of execution used?

C3 What were the long-term effects of the Gunpowder Plot?

How confident do you feel about your answers to these questions? Discuss any you are unsure about with a partner then try rewriting your answers together.

2.4 Witchcraft and the law, c1500–c1700

Key term

Pact*

A formal agreement.

Source A

A woodcut showing three witches and their familiars, c1754

Attitudes to witches, c1500–c1700

At the beginning of this period, in the early 16th century, people of all backgrounds believed in witches. Witches were believed to have made a pact* with the devil in return for special or magical powers – including flying and the ability to make people, or farm animals, sicken and die.

Witches were sometimes identified by their apparent associations with domestic animals. A cat, dog, or even a spider could be a witch's familiar – the devil in the shape of an animal, helping the witch do her evil work.

By the end of this period, c1700, attitudes towards witches were starting to change. They began to be seen as foolish and muddled, or tricksters trying to take advantage of the gullibility of others.

The law on witchcraft

As associates of the devil, it was important to find witches out and punish them. In the Middle Ages, Church courts were used for witchcraft trials and penalties were generally not very severe. However, in 1542, Henry VIII changed the law and witchcraft became a very serious crime that could be punished by death. In 1563, Elizabeth I changed the law so that if a witch tried to kill someone through their witchery, or to raise dead spirits, they would receive the death penalty.

There are a number of reasons why witchcraft came to be viewed and punished more seriously by the authorities:

- During the late 16th century, there were economic problems, including falling wages and rising unemployment. Economic problems increased tensions between people in small communities. The death of livestock, or poor crop yields, were sometimes blamed on evil spirits and witchcraft, rather than bad luck or bad weather conditions.
- The rising fear of vagabonds made richer people increasingly suspicious of the poor – and many accusations of witchcraft were made by wealthy people against poor people.
- After Henry VIII became head of the Church of England, witchcraft was treated as a crime against the king and the state, not just a religious crime.

Laws against witchcraft

Year	Monarch	Law	Effects
1542	Henry VIII	Witchcraft Act	Witchcraft punished by death.
1563	Elizabeth I	Act against Conjurations, Enchantments and Witchcraft	Witchcraft tried in common court, not Church court – common court penalties more severe. Death penalty will be issued when harm caused to another person. Minor witchcraft, using charms and magic, punished by time in the stocks.
1604	James I	Witchcraft and Conjuration Act	Death penalty given to anyone summoning evil spirits.
1735	George II	Witchcraft Act	'Witches' seen as confidence tricksters, and punished with fines and imprisonment.

Religion and witchcraft

As in many other areas of life, religion and the Church played an important part in attitudes to, and definitions of, witchcraft – just as it had during the Middle Ages. Human existence was viewed as a struggle between good and evil – God and the devil.

Some historians argue that when Protestant thinking became more popular – after Henry VIII led the break away from the Catholic Church – people increasingly feared the 'old' religion, Catholicism. This fear led to attempts to 'cleanse' society by seeking out witches.

James I's *Demonologie*

James I was an enthusiastic witch hunter and shared his ideas through a book called *Demonologie*, published in 1597. The book was about the nature of Hell and called witches the 'detestable slaves of the devil'. It set out James's reasons for believing in witches, encouraged readers to find them out, and even included instructions on how to run witch trials. James supported the use of child witnesses in witchcraft trials, even though the law stated that only people aged 14 and over could swear under oath. He also argued that witchcraft was a crime not only against the king, but against God.

When James became King of England in 1603, he published a new edition of *Demonologie*, describing how witches had tried to drown him and his wife during a sea voyage.

In the aftermath of the Gunpowder Plot in 1605, James was extremely fearful of another Catholic rebellion and obsessed with uncovering threats and conspiracies against him. So, he continued to encourage witch hunts.

James's ideas need to be understood in the context of religious unrest at the time, and his genuine fear for his life. His ideas had an important influence on the wider belief in witches at this time.

Social upheaval

The English Civil Wars, which began in 1642, led to massive disruption and uncertainty. Many families were divided, as different members chose to support either the king or parliament. The economic and political chaos of the war years created a climate of fear in which people were more attracted to superstitious* ideas.

> **Key term**
>
> Superstition*
>
> Belief based on old ideas about magic rather than reason or science.

Case study: Matthew Hopkins – Witchfinder General

In 1645, a former Essex lawyer and self-proclaimed 'Witchfinder General' set about the task of hunting down witches in the east of England.

Source B

An illustration from Matthew Hopkins's pamphlet '*The discovery of witches*', published in 1647.

In the 17th century, Justices of the Peace (JPs) were expected to identify religious threats and those who refused to conform to Protestant-led changes in the Church. They were also tasked with finding witches. Matthew Hopkins was employed by a JP in Essex and East Anglia to uncover witchery. There were significant financial rewards, as local magistrates could pay the equivalent of a month's wages for each accused witch.

The Hopkins witchcraft trials

Hopkins used a range of interrogation methods to secure confessions. These included restricting the accused's food to a starvation diet of bread and water, and depriving them of sleep.

In addition, physical evidence was sought by examining the accused's body to look for a 'teat' (nipple), which allowed them to suckle the devil's 'familiars' with their blood. A mole, birthmark or other unusual skin blemish, could all be used as evidence of guilt.

One of Hopkins's techniques ensured that he would always have more witches to try. A full confession was expected to include the names of other witches, supposedly to prove that the accused had truly renounced the devil and was ready to free him- or herself from the devil's influence.

Source C

Extract from the diary of Nehemiah Wallington, describing events in Essex in 1645. Wallington was a strict Puritan who recorded his sins and those of others in extensive notebooks. Here he describes a confession made by Rebecca West.

Shortly after when she was going to bed the Devil appeared unto her again in the shape of a handsome young man, saying that he came to marry her... Asked by the Judge whether she ever had carnal copulation [sex] with the Devil she confessed she had. She was very desirous to confess all she knew, which accordingly she did where upon the rest were apprehended and sent unto the Geole [prison]...

When she looked upon the ground she saw herself encompassed in flames of fire and as soon as she was separated from her mother the tortures and the flames began to cease whereupon she then confessed all she knew... As soon as her confession was fully ended she found her contience [conscience] so satisfied and disburdened of all tortures she thought herself the happiest creature in the world.

Extend your knowledge

Sink or swim

The most notorious method of judging guilt was the 'swimming test' which involved drowning the accused. The guilty would float and the innocent would sink – but, as a result of this method, it was believed that the innocents' souls were saved. This method was unofficial. It was used in some communities, but not demanded by the authorities, and was not used by Hopkins.

Highway robbery was treated as a serious crime because:

- it disrupted travel between towns
- the crime was committed on the king's highway
- it could involve the theft of mail bags and so disrupted the postal service.

In 1772, in an effort to clamp down on the activities of highwaymen, the death penalty was introduced for anyone found armed and in disguise on a high road. Highway robbery continued into the 19th century, but after 1815 the crime became less common. The last reported case was in 1831.

One important factor contributing to the decrease in highway robbery was the use of mounted patrols on major roads in the 19th century. Another was the growth of the banking system, as it meant there was less need for people to carry large sums in cash.

Extend your knowledge

Highwaymen – heroes and villains

Highwaymen were hugely popular, despite the fact they committed violent crime. In 1724, thousands of admirers lined the street, from Newgate Prison to the gallows at Tyburn, to see the highwayman Jack Shepherd being taken to his execution. The onlookers threw flowers, and public houses gave out free pints of beer. Shepherd had been imprisoned and escaped four times, which led to his fame. He was so popular that, after his death, the authorities banned any plays that included his name in the title. The highwayman Dick Turpin is also remembered in fiction and legend as a brave and glamorous hero – although he committed many violent assaults and robberies.

Exam-style question, Section B

Why did the problem of highway robbery increase and decrease in the period 1700–1900?

You may use the following in your answer:

- increased wealth
- the death penalty

You **must** include information of your own.

12 marks

Exam tip

This question tests understanding of key features and causation. First focus on factors that help explain **why** highway robbery came about, and then on factors that led to its decline. Try to make links between the factors.

Poaching: continuity and change

Poaching continued to be a widespread crime after 1700 and, as with smuggling, there was a rise in gangs operating on a large scale. Poaching raids prompted the authorities to make anti-poaching laws harsher. The 1723 Black Act was passed to try to deal with these gangs, by making poaching a capital offence. The act also made it illegal to blacken your face (a form of disguise) in a hunting area, and carrying snares, or even owning dogs that were suitable for poaching, could be punished by fines or a prison sentence.

Anti-poaching laws were heavily resented because they were viewed as unfair. Only landowners with land worth over £100 a year were allowed to hunt without restrictions. In 1823, the Black Act was repealed as part of a large number of legal reforms led by Robert Peel (see page 97). Poaching was still illegal but would no longer be punishable by death.

The decriminalisation of witchcraft

In 1736, during the reign of George II, a new Witchcraft Act was passed. This decriminalised witchcraft. People no longer believed in witches and witchcraft and those who claimed to be 'witches' were now seen as confidence tricksters trying to take advantage of others. The new act set out much less severe punishments of fines and imprisonments than people accused of witchcraft had faced in the past.

The Tolpuddle martyrs

A revolution in France, in 1789, had led to a temporary overthrow of the ruling classes, with thousands of members of the nobility executed. There were further popular uprisings in France in 1830. This made the authorities in Britain feel vulnerable, and contributed to them treating those who wanted political change as criminals.

The case of the Tolpuddle martyrs* shows how the government dealt with threats to authority at this time, and how changing attitudes could influence the government's approach to, and definitions of, crime.

Key term

Martyr*

A person who suffers for their beliefs and, often, is admired for it.

In February 1834, in the village of Tolpuddle in Dorset, a farm labourer called George Loveless was arrested as he was leaving for work. He and five others – Loveless's brother James, James Brine, James Hammett, Thomas Standfield and his son John – were accused of 'administering an illegal oath'. They had broken an old law intended to stop sailors in the Navy organising mutinies.

However, the real motive for their arrest was to stop their political activities. The men had sworn to do what they could to protect their wages and help each other. They had also formed a 'friendly society', an early form of trade union*. They wanted to protest about their low wages: six shillings a week, when the average wage for a farm labourer was ten shillings a week.

Key term

Trade union*

An organisation that represents workers to protect their rights.

Extend your knowledge

A time of change

Rapid urbanisation and industrialisation, at the end of the 18th and beginning of the 19th centuries, meant that many workers lived in poor conditions, working for low wages and with no legal protection as workers. As a result, some working people demanded changes to the political system, including the right to vote and the right to go on strike. Some workers formed trade unions to campaign collectively for greater rights and improved conditions. The authorities were concerned that this could lead to too much power in the hands of the workers.

Source C

This article about the trial of the Tolpuddle martyrs is from the *Caledonian Mercury* newspaper, published 29 March 1834.

TRADES' UNIONS.—At the Dorchester Assizes on Monday, six labourers, named J. Loveless, J. Loveless, T. Stanfield, J. Stanfield, J. Hammett, and J. Brine, were indicted under the 57th Geo. III. c. 19, sec. 25, for having administered an unlawful oath to John Lock. The prisoners belonged to the "Friendly Society of Agricultural Labourers," which contained provisions among its rules, that if any master attempted to reduce the wages of his workmen, those who were members of the society should quit, and that no member should divulge any of the secrets, or violate the same; and that if he did, his crime would be communicated to all the lodges in the country, and he would be hunted from the society of the Unionists. Two men, named Lock and Legg, gave evidence that they had joined the Union, and that they were blindfolded in a room at a house in Tolpuddle, and sworn to strike for wages when others did, and to wish that their "souls might be plunged into eternity" if they divulged the secrets of the order. After the ceremony, the handkerchief was removed from their eyes, and they were told to look on the picture of a skeleton, some one exclaiming at the time, "Remember your end." Mr Baron Williams said, that if the Jury were satisfied that the oath was intended as an obligation on the conscience of the person taking it, it came within the meaning of the act, and the prisoners must be found guilty. The Jury returned a verdict of *Guilty*, and all the prisoners were sentenced to be transported for seven years.

suitable alternative punishment for offenders. Common views about prison were that:

- it was an opportunity to change or rehabilitate a person who had committed crime
- as well as punishing criminals, a prison term should deter others from crime
- prison sentences should involve hard work to pay back society
- prison made society safer by separating criminals from everyone else.

Not everyone agreed on whether the main purpose of prison should be rehabilitation or punishment. Those who favoured punishment thought prisoners should be kept in harsh conditions and perform hard labour. A common form of hard labour was the treadwheel: the prisoner walked up the wheel for ten minutes at a time, with a five-minute break before the next ten-minute stint. This went on for eight hours a day, and prisoners climbed the equivalent of over 2.5 km in every shift. Prisoners stood in separate booths at the wheel to ensure there was no communication between them. Power generated by the treadwheel was sometimes used in the prison, for example for pumping water.

Prison reformers generally thought that the main purpose of prison should be rehabilitation. Two of the most influential reformers were John Howard and Elizabeth Fry.

Source D

A row of treadwheels at Pentonville Prison, photographed in 1895.

Howard is outraged by conditions in the Bedfordshire county gaol.

Concerned that some prisoners were detained as they could not afford their release fee so in 1774 he campaigns to persuade parliament to ensure that prisoners who have finished their sentences are released.

Tours other prisons, looking for good examples to remodel the gaol on and writes down what he sees at each prison. Almost everywhere, conditions are bad. In 1777, publishes *The State of Prisons in England and Wales*, providing detailed evidence for other prison reformers.

Howard believes that criminals will only change their ways if given a reasonable standard of living in prison.

Recommends clean, decent food and water, useful work, Christian teaching, private cells to allow reflection on crimes, a wage for gaolers so they won't exploit prisoners.

Makes visits to individual gaolers around the country to persuade them to improve their practices.

John Howard
Born in London, 1726. Appointed as High Sheriff of Bedfordshire in 1773. As High Sheriff he is responsible for the county gaol.

Aged 18 Fry starts doing charity work, helping the poor, sick and prisoners.

In 1813, visits Newgate prison and is shocked by the conditions. Some prisoners have been detained without trial. Women and children live alongside dangerous prisoners in filthy, overcrowded conditions.

Teaches sewing and leads Bible classes at Newgate to encourage rehabilitation.

In 1817, helps set up the Association for the Reformation of Female Prisoners at Newgate to campaign for better conditions.

Helps ensure that female warders are employed to work with female and child prisoners.

Organises prison education for women and children at Newgate.

Improves living conditions, providing prisoners with furniture and clothing.

Writes letters and campaigns for wider prison reform.

Elizabeth Fry
Born in Norfolk, 1780. Prison reformer.

Figure 3.2 The prison reformers John Howard and Elizabeth Fry.

Growing government involvement

During this period, the government became increasingly involved in the organisation and running of the prison system. See Section 3.4, to find out more about how the new rules were applied at Pentonville Prison.

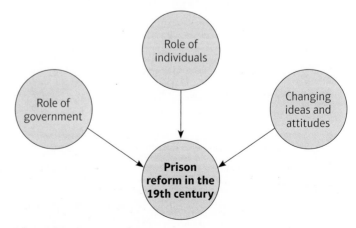

Figure 3.3 Factors influencing prison reform in the 19th century.

Timeline
Reorganising the prison system, 1815–77

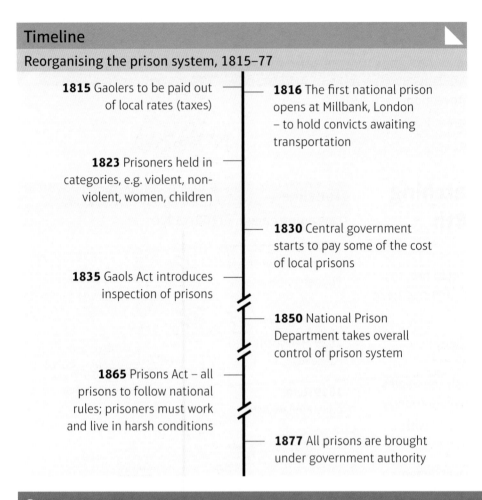

1815 Gaolers to be paid out of local rates (taxes)

1816 The first national prison opens at Millbank, London – to hold convicts awaiting transportation

1823 Prisoners held in categories, e.g. violent, non-violent, women, children

1830 Central government starts to pay some of the cost of local prisons

1835 Gaols Act introduces inspection of prisons

1850 National Prison Department takes overall control of prison system

1865 Prisons Act – all prisons to follow national rules; prisoners must work and live in harsh conditions

1877 All prisons are brought under government authority

Summary
- During the early part of the 19th century, the Bloody Code was questioned by those who believed more effective punishments should be found for less serious crimes.
- Transportation to Australia was a serious punishment and was seen as an effective deterrent.
- Reformers, like Charles Dickens, questioned whether public execution of criminals was an effective deterrent and led campaigns to change opinions.
- The growth of the prison system meant an alternative punishment to transportation was available.

Checkpoint
Strengthen
S1 List three changes to prisons that were campaigned for by Elizabeth Fry.

S2 Write down three factors that influenced the decline of the Bloody Code.

Challenge
C1 In what ways did criticisms of transportation differ in Australia and Britain?

C2 Explain why either Elizabeth Fry or John Howard was an important figure in the reform of punishments.

C3 Was the end of public execution more the result of humanitarianism, or of demands for more effective punishments? Make notes to support both arguments.

How confident do you feel about your answers to these questions? Reread the section, making notes as you go. Now try answering the questions again.

Crime prevention and catching criminals in the early 18th century

In the early 18th century, the law continued to be enforced using a combination of methods that had been used previously. These included:

- parish constables who dealt with disorderly behaviour, petty criminals and beggars
- watchmen, who were organised by parish constables and were responsible for protecting private property
- part-time soldiers who were used to dealing with rebellions or riots.

Some towns had salaried constables and watchmen, so in these places some features of a modern police force were already present. For example, there were regular foot-patrols by men who were employed to prevent crime and arrest suspects. They were more experienced than the part-time householders they replaced, but they were low-paid and the job had a low status. Some people were concerned that paid watchmen and constables had too close a relationship with the criminals they were supposed to police.

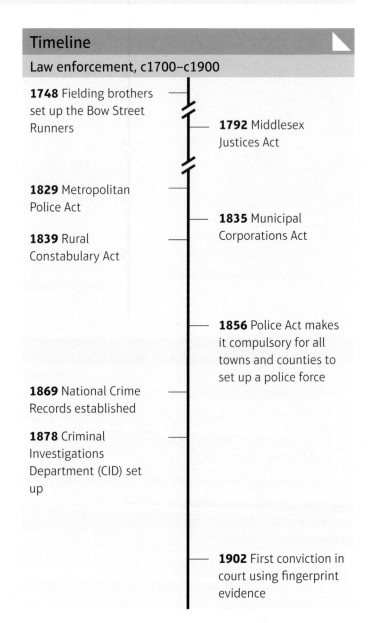

Timeline

Law enforcement, c1700–c1900

1748 Fielding brothers set up the Bow Street Runners

1792 Middlesex Justices Act

1829 Metropolitan Police Act

1835 Municipal Corporations Act

1839 Rural Constabulary Act

1856 Police Act makes it compulsory for all towns and counties to set up a police force

1869 National Crime Records established

1878 Criminal Investigations Department (CID) set up

1902 First conviction in court using fingerprint evidence

Origins of the Bow Street Runners, 1748

Source A

A popular print, published in 1806, showing the Bow Street Runners catching criminals.

The Bow Street Runners were a crime-fighting team, established in London, in 1748, by the Chief Magistrate, Henry Fielding, who had offices at Bow Street.

Initially, Henry Fielding used a small team of volunteers to attend crime scenes and detect criminals. He was convinced that 'thief takers' (see page 52) should form a part of law enforcement, but also recognised they needed to be reformed and monitored to improve their effectiveness and questionable reputation. He appointed thief takers as 'principal officers' – who became known as Bow Street Runners. He also published descriptions of wanted persons in the local *Covent Garden Journal*.

In 1754, Henry's brother, John Fielding, took over the Bow Street Runners. At first the Fieldings charged fees for their services, and collected rewards from the victims of crime if successful convictions were secured. But by 1785, the Bow Street Runners were officially paid by the government and were the first modern detective force.

Significance of the Bow Street Runners

The Fielding brothers' approach was innovative in a number of ways:

- Their objective was to deter criminals by increasing the chances of them being caught and successfully prosecuted.
- They organised regular foot and horse patrols, by paid constables, along major roads.
- They understood the importance of collecting and sharing information about crime and suspects with other law enforcers. Their Bow Street office became a hub for a crime intelligence network.

The success of the Bow Street Runners led to more detective offices being set up in Middlesex and Westminster. In 1792, the Middlesex Justices Act set up further offices, each with six constables tasked with the job of detecting and arresting suspects.

Developments in police forces in the 19th century

The mixture of part-time constables, watchmen and Bow Street Runners was not sufficient to deal properly with law and order. But there was still strong opposition to the idea of a consolidated police force:

- Some people were worried about their personal freedoms and privacy.
- Some doubted it would really make a difference to law and order.
- Opponents thought it would be too expensive to fund.

Turning point: London's first professional police force, 1829

In 1829, England's first professional police force was established in London. The Metropolitan Police Act gave London a uniformed police force. Seventeen districts across London each had its own police division, with four inspectors and 144 constables. The emphasis was on deterring criminals by having a public presence on the street, with constables patrolling their beats to counter crime and catch any criminals that were 'caught in the act'. This new police force had far greater numbers than the Bow Street Runners and was better organised.

The Home Secretary, Robert Peel, was keen to ensure that the police force was viewed in a positive light, so they had a uniform of blue overcoats and top hats to identify them and distinguish them from the army. Despite Peel's attempts to make the new police force acceptable to the public, there was significant public concern that they could be used to prevent political protest or put down opposition to the government. For more on Robert Peel's reforms see Section 3.5.

Developments in police forces, 1829–56

Improvements in policing outside London were slow and by the mid-19th century there were still big differences between regions. While some areas had professional police forces, many still relied on the old system of parish constables.

The pace of change was slow for a number of reasons:

- The public were concerned about the potential costs involved.
- There was no co-operation between different areas.
- Development was optional, rather than enforceable by central government, so many local government organisations simply didn't bother with the reforms.

Developments in police forces, 1856–1900

The 1856 Police Act meant that all areas now had to have a professional police force that was centrally controlled. All police forces were now inspected by government officials and only received government financial grants if they were delivering their policing services efficiently. The act also established the principle of deterrence through detection of criminals – the idea that criminals would be less likely to commit crimes if they knew police officers were actively looking for them.

In 1869, the first National Crime Records were set up. This saw the use of new technology in policing. Telegraph communications meant that different police forces could communicate quickly and effectively to share information about crimes and suspects.

Crime detection and the start of the CID

In 1842, a regular detective branch was established at Scotland Yard with 16 officers. Instead of patrolling the beat in uniform, they focused on investigating crimes and wore ordinary 'plain clothes'. Their activities were viewed by some with suspicion, and accusations that they were no better than spies on the public.

Later, in 1878, the Criminal Investigations Department (CID) was set up. This employed 200 detectives. A further 600 were added in 1883. The CID developed new methods of detection. In the 1880s, they tried to identify Jack the Ripper by his handwriting in 1902 they secured the conviction of a burglar using fingerprint evidence left at the crime scene.

Act	Measure	Impact
1835 Municipal Corporations Act	Gave borough councils powers to set up a local police force.	Only 93 out of 171 had done so by 1837.
1839 Rural Constabulary Act	Allowed the 54 counties to organise a paid police force in their area. JPs were given powers to appoint chief constables and employ one police constable per 1,000 population.	Only 36 counties did so by 1850.
1856 Police Act	Forced the entire country to set up local police forces.	Start of the modern police service.

Exam-style question, Section B

Explain one way in which policing was similar in Tudor England and the early 18th century.   **4 marks**

Exam tip

This question tests knowledge and understanding of key features and similarities and differences. Remember to give one way that policing was the same and support this with information from both periods.

Summary

- Early 18th century law enforcement continued to use methods similar to the early modern period.
- The Bow Street Runners were established in 1748, marking an important development in policing.
- In 1829, England's first professional police force, the Metropolitan Police, was established in London.
- The 1856 Police Act meant that all areas had to have a professional police force that was centrally controlled by government.
- In 1878, the Criminal Investigations Department was set up.

Checkpoint

Strengthen

S1 List three ways in which policing at the start of the 18th century was similar to the 16th century.

S2 Describe the impact of two new laws on policing across England.

Challenge

C1 Explain why the shift towards detection, rather than just deterrence, marks an important change in policing.

C2 Why were changes in approaches to policing slow and varied in this period?

C3 How was technology used to improve police methods at this time?

C4 Why was the public initially hostile towards the Criminal Investigation Department?

How confident do you feel about your answers to these questions? Form a small group, discuss the answers, then rewrite improved answers in your group.

3.4 Case study: The separate system at Pentonville Prison

Timeline
Development of prisons in the 19th century

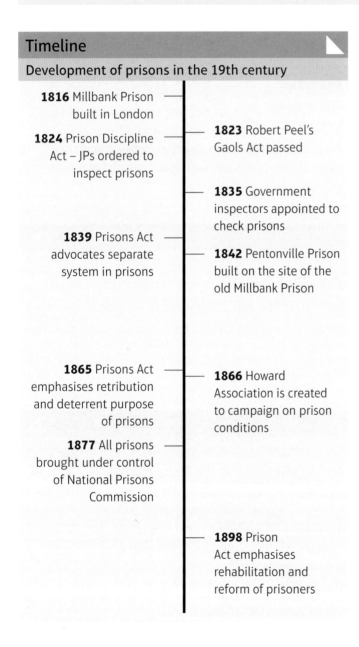

1816 Millbank Prison built in London

1823 Robert Peel's Gaols Act passed

1824 Prison Discipline Act – JPs ordered to inspect prisons

1835 Government inspectors appointed to check prisons

1839 Prisons Act advocates separate system in prisons

1842 Pentonville Prison built on the site of the old Millbank Prison

1865 Prisons Act emphasises retribution and deterrent purpose of prisons

1866 Howard Association is created to campaign on prison conditions

1877 All prisons brought under control of National Prisons Commission

1898 Prison Act emphasises rehabilitation and reform of prisoners

Key term

Prototype*

A new idea or design that is tried out before more versions are made.

The growth of the prison system in the mid 19th century

The Victorians were increasingly worried about rising crime rates: between 1800 and 1840 the number of crimes reported per year had risen from 5,000 to 20,000. In the 18th century, prison was not generally used as a punishment in its own right; but, through the 19th century, prison was increasingly seen as a viable alternative to transportation and execution. The era of private prisons with desperately poor conditions was ending, and reformers argued for a system that was tough, but not bad for prisoners' health.

The separate system at Pentonville Prison

Pentonville Prison was built in 1842 as a prototype* where the 'separate system' could be tested. Under this system, prisoners were kept apart as much as possible. They lived in separate cells and stayed there for up to 23 hours a day. Separate conditions were intended to:

- provide prisoners with an opportunity for individual improvement
- give prisoners solitude to encourage reform through religious faith and self-reflection
- ensure prisoners were not influenced by other criminals who might encourage them to commit even worse crimes
- deter people from committing crimes because of the serious nature of the punishment
- ensure retribution – making the criminal 'pay' for their behaviour by being punished.

The building

Every aspect of the new prison was designed to support the separate system. The building had five wings with a base for staff in the central area. Each wing was made up of dozens of individual cells, and altogether the prison could accommodate 520 prisoners.

The cells had a floor area of just 4m by 2m. There was a small high window at the end to allow some natural daylight in. The windows had thick glass and were fixed with iron bars for extra security.

The prison had a heating system and a mechanical ventilation system; and the cells featured some of the most up-to-date domestic technology, including piped water to each cell, a small basin for washing and a basic toilet. These measures were put in place to improve the health and living conditions of the prisoners, but also ensured that they would not have the chance to see or speak to each other, as they had no need to leave their cells.

Extend your knowledge

Joshua Jebb, Prison Surveyor General

Jebb was appointed Prison Surveyor General by the Home Office. He designed Pentonville as a 'model' prison in 1840–42. With a background in engineering, he ensured that the building included modern features such as ventilation, heating and piped water. Between 1842 and 1877, 90 new prisons were built or extended using the design ideas that Jebb introduced at Pentonville.

Source A

Architect's plans for the design of Pentonville Prison, 1842.

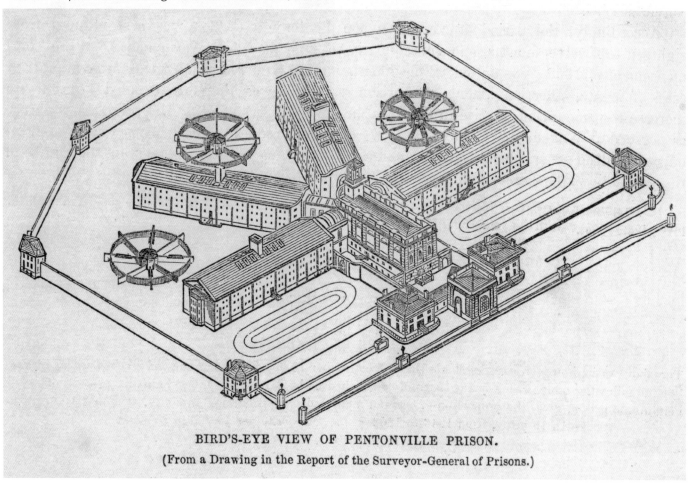

BIRD'S-EYE VIEW OF PENTONVILLE PRISON.
(From a Drawing in the Report of the Surveyor-General of Prisons.)

The living conditions

Living conditions in Pentonville were highly disciplined. The early ideas behind the separate system were focused on isolating prisoners to ensure that they had time to face up to their crimes. Every feature of the prison was designed to add to their isolation:

- The building's walls were thick to stop prisoners communicating between cells.
- Initially, prisoners worked in their cells to ensure they remained isolated through the day. The work was deliberately very boring and repetitive: for example, oakum picking, which involved unravelling and cleaning old rope.
- Prisoners were allowed out for a short period of exercise or to go to chapel, but there were elaborate systems in place to stop them from speaking to, or even seeing, one another. They wore face masks for exercise, and in chapel they sat in individual cubicles wearing masks made of brown sacking.

The solitary conditions and lack of human contact meant many prisoners suffered from mental illness, including depression and psychosis*. There was also a high rate of suicide.

Key word

Psychosis*

A confused state where sufferers have hallucinations and delusions – seeing and imagining things that are not really there.

Source C

Prisoners at Pentonville during an outdoor exercise session. Face masks ensured that time outside their cells was still as isolated as possible.

Source B

Separate cell at Pentonville Prison 1842. The cell housed a hammock-style bed and a mattress with a blanket. This cell had a weaving loom so the inmate could work without leaving the room.

SEPARATE CELL IN PENTONVILLE PRISON.
WITH HAMMOCK SLUNG FOR SLEEPING, AND LOOM FOR DAY-WORK.

Activities ?

1. List three methods used by the authorities to keep Pentonville inmates separate from each other.
2. Why were prisoners made to do boring and repetitive work?

Views of the separate system

Some prison reformers, including Elizabeth Fry, were concerned about the purpose and design of Pentonville Prison as a future model for other prisons. Reformers wanted prisoners to have the opportunity to change their ways and be rehabilitated, so that they would change for the better on their release from prison. The separate system could be used in this way, but many people in government were more concerned with deterring potential criminals and punishing wrongdoing, rather than rehabilitating prisoners.

Elizabeth Fry raised her concerns about the impact of the separate system with government authorities, including the Prison Surveyor General, Joshua Jebb.

Source D

From a letter written by Elizabeth Fry to Joshua Jebb, on the subject of Pentonville Prison, in 1841.

These cells appear to me calculated to excite such an awful terror in the mind... I am certain that separate confinement produces an unhealthy state, both of mind and body, and that, therefore everything should be done to counteract [balance] this influence... I consider light, air and the power of seeing something beyond the mere monotonous walls of a cell, highly important.

Activities ?

1 Summarise the points that Elizabeth Fry makes in her letter in Source D.

2 Why does she think that conditions at Pentonville could harm prisoners?

3 Write a letter from Joshua Jebb, in reply to Elizabeth Fry, covering each of the points she raises.

The late 19th century: increasingly harsh treatment of prisoners

In the latter half of the 19th century the regime at Pentonville Prison, and other prisons around the country, became harsher. The aim of the 1865 Prisons Act was to enforce a strict, uniform regime of punishment in all prisons. It did not aim to reform prisoners through religious faith or work.

The Assistant Director of Prisons, Sir Edmund Du Cane, declared that prisoners would get 'Hard labour, hard fare and hard board'. This meant:

- hard labour: physically demanding work for up to 12 hours every day
- hard fare: a deliberately boring and bland diet, with the same food served on the same day every week
- hard board: wooden board beds instead of the hammocks prisoners had slept on previously.

Source E

The writer Oscar Wilde was held in Pentonville Prison in 1898. This is an extract from a letter he wrote to the *Daily Chronicle* newspaper, urging reforms of the system.

Deprived of books, of all human intercourse [conversation], isolated from every humane and humanising influence, condemned to eternal silence... treated like an unintelligent animal... the wretched man who is confined in an English prison can hardly escape becoming insane.

Summary

- Pentonville was a prototype or model prison. The main concern for the authorities was to keep prisoners as separate as possible.
- The government was concerned with punishing wrongdoing and deterring others from crime by ensuring conditions were sufficiently harsh.
- In the latter half of the 19th century, the regime at Pentonville Prison became harsher.
- The aim of the 1865 Prisons Act was to enforce a strict, uniform regime of punishment in all prisons – not to reform prisoners.

Checkpoint

Strengthen

S1 Describe three aspects of the separate system that led prisoners to suffer mental illness.

S2 Why were inmates forced to do work like oakum picking?

S3 What was the purpose of making convicts do hard labour like climbing the treadwheel?

Challenge

C1 Do you think that hard labour would have made a prisoner change their behaviour after they were released from prison?

C2 How did the prison system become more severe from the 1860s?

C3 Why was Pentonville Prison criticised by some prison reformers?

How confident do you feel about your answers to these questions? If you're not sure you answered them well, discuss the answers with a partner and record your conclusions. Your teacher can give you some hints.

Aims include:

- helping the police prevent crime, by encouraging local vigilance*
- reducing fear of crime, by increasing community involvement
- reporting crime trends to the police.

In the early 1980s, the number of local Neighbourhood Watches rose from 1,000 to 29,000, but there was a lot of controversy over whether this initiative was effective in preventing crime.

Origins of Neighbourhood Watch

During the 1980s the prime minister, Margaret Thatcher, led a Conservative government that wanted to increase the role and responsibility of the individual, and reduce the role of the state. In crime prevention the idea of active citizenship* was promoted as part of this government policy. Unlike community law enforcement from earlier periods, like the 'hue and cry', this system was entirely voluntary.

Neighbourhood Watch was imported as an idea from the US where it was originally set up in Chicago and was believed to be successful in tackling crime.

Britain in the early 1980s saw a dramatic increase in crimes and society was keen to see the implementation of new ways to reduce it.

> **Key term**
>
> **Vigilance***
>
> Keeping a careful watch for danger or possible criminal activity.

> **Key term**
>
> **Active citizenship***
>
> People taking an active role in their community in order to improve it.

> **Source E**
>
> Sign showing that residents in this area participate in a Neighbourhood Watch scheme.

> **Source F**
>
> Bill Pitt MP, speaking about the Neighbourhood Watch scheme in a House of Commons debate on 28 February 1983.
>
> We have reached a crux. Crime is growing and we are seen as losing the battle as Sir Kenneth Newman says... I welcome his suggestion that the community should play its part in conquering crime. I welcome the neighbourhood watch. I had strong reservations... because I wondered whether some people would set up vigilante [private individual who takes the law into their own hands to prevent crime] groups.

Source G

From the Police Commissioner, Sir Kenneth Newman's, Annual Report for 1986.

We have always sought public co-operation, but in the past we have relied largely on exhortation [sending encouraging messages]. Over the last four years, however, we have been deliberately organising a coherent structure within which the public will be enabled to work with us in a purposeful manner. The building blocks so far are consultative groups, neighbourhood watch schemes, business watch schemes, victim support schemes, crime prevention panels and estate policing projects. Neighbourhood Watch has increased the commitment of members to the quality of life in their neighbourhood.

Public attitudes towards Neighbourhood Watch schemes

Some people believed the scheme made a significant and positive change. Others claimed that the system was ineffective and did not prevent crime.

Activities

1 What does Bill Pitt say, in Source F, about the reasons why Neighbourhood Watch was needed?

2 What concerns did Bill Pitt have about the impact of Neighbourhood Watch schemes?

3 In what ways does Kenneth Newman, in Source G, claim that Neighbourhood Watch schemes were different to the previous relationship between the police and the local community?

Exam-style question, Section B

Explain one way that the system of community law enforcement in the 20th century was different from community law enforcement in the 16th century.

4 marks

Exam tip

This question tests knowledge and understanding of key features and difference. Remember to give one way community law enforcement in the 20th century was different from the 16th century system and then add details from both periods to show the difference.

Figure 4.2 Some common views of the Neighbourhood Watch scheme in the 1980s.

Summary

- Important developments in modern policing include increased use of science and technology, more emphasis on crime prevention, and increasing co-ordination and co-operation at a national level.
- In the 20th century there was increasing specialisation in police forces, with special divisions set up and better training.
- There was an increasing emphasis on crime prevention, including voluntary Neighbourhood Watch schemes.

Checkpoint

Strengthen

S1 Describe three new uses of technology introduced by the police in the 20th century.

S2 What is the role of forensic investigators?

S3 Describe two ways that the police work alongside local communities to prevent crime.

Challenge

C1 How has technology helped the police to focus more on crime prevention?

C2 Why was Neighbourhood Watch introduced in the 1980s?

How confident do you feel about your answers to these questions? Form a small group and discuss any questions you are not sure about. Look for the answers in this section. Now rewrite your answers as a group.

4.3 Changes in punishment, c1900–present

Learning outcomes

- Understand why the death penalty was abolished in the 20th century.
- Know about changes to the prison system, including specialised treatment of young prisoners and greater emphasis on rehabilitation.

Abolition of the death penalty

From Anglo-Saxon Britain to the 20th century, execution was used as the ultimate punishment. However, it was used less and less from the beginning of the 19th century, and by the 1830s murder and treason were the only crimes punished with the death penalty. Throughout the 19th century, politicians attempted to introduce new laws to end the death penalty, but they were unsuccessful.

At the start of the 20th century, capital punishment was still used – usually for the crime of murder. However, during this period, attitudes in society were changing, and a range of laws were introduced that meant the death penalty had been abolished* by the mid 20th century.

Key term

Abolished*

Banned or made illegal.

In the early 1950s, around 15 people a year were executed. However, the Homicide Act of 1957 restricted the death penalty to the most serious cases of murder, which were known as capital murders (see Extend your knowledge on the next page). After 1957, there was an average of four executions per year.

In 1965, the Murder Act suspended the death penalty for murder for five years. This decision was made permanent with an amendment to the act in 1969. A few crimes continued to carry the death penalty, including: espionage, arson in the royal dockyards, and piracy with violence; but the death penalty was not used for these crimes, and these were gradually added to the list of crimes that would not be punished by death. The death penalty was ended for all crimes in 1998.

Timeline

Decreasing use of the death penalty in the 20th century

1908 Children's Act ends hanging of under-16s

1922 Infanticide Act passed – mothers who kill newborn babies will no longer receive death penalty

1933 Hanging of under-18s ends

1949 Royal Commission on Capital Punishment set up

1956 Death Penalty (Abolition) Bill passed by House of Commons – but rejected by House of Lords

1957 Homicide Act limits death sentence to five categories of murder

1965 Death penalty abolished for most crimes

1998 High treason and piracy with violence no longer punishable by death

1999 Home secretary signs 6th protocol of European Convention on Human Rights – formally ending the death penalty in Britain

Activity ?

'The abolition of capital punishment was a gradual process'. Use three events from the timeline to explain this statement.

Source A

A newspaper headline announcing the abolition of capital punishment.

When the death penalty was eventually abolished in 1965, the home secretary was Roy Jenkins. He had strong views about ending the death penalty, and his influence is often seen as playing a key role in this change in the law.

Changing attitudes

During the 20th century, children were increasingly shown more tolerance in the law. It was recognised that children did not have the same understanding of their actions as adults, so they should not be punished as severely. In 1908, the Children's Act said that under-16s could no longer be sentenced to death. Following the Young Person's Act of 1933 the age limit was raised to 18. The same act set the age of criminal responsibility* at eight years old. This was raised to ten years old in 1963.

Additionally, the Infanticide Act, passed in 1922, said that women would not be punished with the death penalty if they killed a child shortly after its birth. This more lenient treatment of women was due to increasing understanding that a woman's mental state could be affected by pregnancy and childbirth.

During the 1960s, the British government passed laws on a range of social issues that reflected a wider change in attitudes (see Section 4.1). Overall, the pace of change in the development of more liberal* attitudes to punishment was greater in Britain, in the 20th century, than it ever had been before.

The role of government

In parliament, opinions about the death penalty were strongly divided. The House of Commons passed bills abolishing the death penalty in 1948 and 1956 – but these were blocked by the House of Lords.

Interpretation 1

From an article by Liz Homans, published in *History Today* in 2008.

At 8am on August 13th, 1964, Peter Allen and Gwynne Evans were hanged — Evans at Strangeways in Manchester, Allen at Walton Prison in Liverpool. They were the respective hangmen's last jobs. The following year Parliament voted to abolish the death penalty. This reform is often seen as emblematic [a symbol] of the 1960s, part of a shift towards a more 'permissive' [open and tolerant] society. However, the abolition of capital punishment did not reflect any sea change in public opinion, which remained firmly opposed to abolition. For abolitionists, the vote had nothing to do with any permissive society; it was the successful end of a long, long campaign.

Controversial executions

In the 1950s, a series of controversial executions caused the public to question the death penalty more and more, and led to protests about the use of capital punishment. For more detail on the Derek Bentley trial, and its influence on the end of capital punishment, see Section 4.5.

1950	Timothy Evans	Hanged for murdering his wife and baby. Later evidence proved that they had been killed by a serial killer and Evans was innocent. There was a huge public outcry at the miscarriage of justice.
1953	Derek Bentley	Hanged for murder of a police officer. Bentley had learning difficulties and a low mental age. He had not fired the gun himself but was prosecuted nonetheless.
1955	Ruth Ellis	Hanged for the murder of her violent and abusive boyfriend. He had attacked her when she was pregnant and caused her to miscarry. Ellis was also the mother of a young child who was orphaned by her mother's execution. A petition, with 50,000 signatures asking for leniency, was ignored by the home secretary.

Source B

Crowds outside Holloway Prison, protesting about the execution of Ruth Ellis on 13 July 1955.

Activities

1. For each of the three cases in the table, explain why the use of the death penalty led to public opposition.

2. Look at Interpretation 1. Does Homans believe that the death penalty was abolished because of more liberal attitudes in society, or because politicians were determined to abolish the death penalty **despite** public opinion?

Changes in the prison system

The use of prison as a punishment has continued to increase since 1900. During the 20th century, ideas about the purpose of prison, and the type of treatment prisoners should expect, changed. The current cost of keeping a person in prison for a year is estimated at £40,000, and reoffending rates are very high. Therefore, questions continue to be asked about the use of prison as a punishment in modern society.

Year	New idea	Practical outcomes
1896	Mentally ill prisoners treated separately to other prisoners.	Broadmoor Hospital opened.
1902	Hard labour ended.	No more treadwheels in prison.
1907	Alternatives to prisons used.	Probation officers employed to check on offenders living outside prison.
1922	Increased focus on prisoner welfare.	Separate system of prisoners ended. New initiatives to improve conditions. Educational opportunities introduced.
1933	New focus on preparing prisoners for life after serving their sentence.	First open prison at New Hall, Wakefield. Open prisons offered a more relaxed regime. Prisoners were allowed out on day release to work and prepare for reintegration into society.

Source C

Vicky Pryce describes her experience of East Sutton Park open prison in an article published on the *Daily Mail* website in October 2013.

It was a far cry from what we had left behind. Even so, I was astonished to discover that Friday night was karaoke night in the pool room between 8.30 and 10.30 – which I went to on my first night. Saturday night was bingo night, for which you had to pay a fee of 50p, and bedtime was 11pm on weekdays and midnight on the weekends.

The Right-wing call for tougher regimes forgets one fact: for these women losing their liberty and their families is the most horrific thing to happen to them.

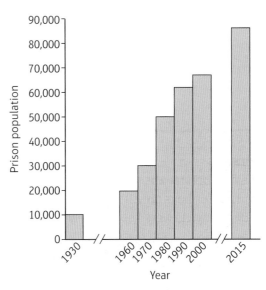

Figure 4.3 The UK prison population, 1930–2015.

Specialised treatment of young offenders

Since 1900, the treatment of young people who break the law has been affected by changing social attitudes, key individuals, and different political ideas put forward by government.

Treatment of young offenders in the 20th century

1900 Borstals introduced

1933 Age of criminal responsibility raised to eight

1948 Criminal Justice Act passed

1963 Age of criminal responsibility raised to ten

1969 Specialised juvenile courts, care orders and supervision orders introduced

1983 Youth custody and youth detention centres replace prison and borstal for under 21s

Borstals

The first borstal was set up in Kent in 1902. This was a prison for boys only. Its purpose was to ensure that young convicts were kept entirely separate from older criminals.

In 1908, the Prevention of Crime Act created a national system of borstals. Those who designed the new system wanted borstals to emphasise education rather than punishment. The day was very structured and disciplined, and inmates took part in physical exercise, and education and work programmes that focused on learning practical skills. Some estimates suggest

that reoffending rates were about 30% in the 1930s, compared to about 60% in the present day.

In 1982, the Criminal Justice Act abolished the borstal system and replaced borstals with youth custody centres.

Source D

Boys exercising at a borstal in 1937.

Youth justice reforms in the 1940s

The Labour government, which came to power after the Second World War, introduced many radical welfare and social reforms. These included reforms to the youth justice system. The Criminal Justice Act of 1948 reduced the use of prison for juveniles, and led to improvements in the probation service for young people.

Reforms introduced by the 1948 Criminal Justice Act included:

- a graduated system of prison, depending on the seriousness of the crime and the offender's record
- detention centres being introduced as a deterrent for young offenders – with a more relaxed regime compared to borstals
- attendance centres being used for young people who had committed minor crimes – young offenders attended the centres at weekends for rehabilitation, instead of being detained all week.

Individuals were also important in making changes. Between 1922 and 1947, a prisons commissioner called Alexander Patterson was influential in changing how young offenders were treated. The 1948 Criminal Justice

Source D

First World War postcard portraying COs as scared to fight and not 'real men'.

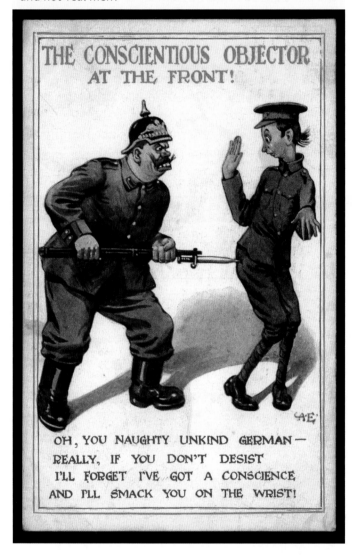

THE CONSCIENTIOUS OBJECTOR AT THE FRONT!

OH, YOU NAUGHTY UNKIND GERMAN —
REALLY, IF YOU DON'T DESIST
I'LL FORGET I'VE GOT A CONSCIENCE
AND I'LL SMACK YOU ON THE WRIST!

Key terms

Propaganda*

Deliberate mass persuasion.

Peace Pledge Union*

An organisation founded in the 1930s that opposed war and sought to find peaceful means to resolve conflicts around the world.

Changes in treatment of COs during the Second World War

During the Second World War (1939–45), COs were offered alternative occupations such as farm work. Prison was generally used as a last resort rather than as a standard deterrent to other potential objectors. However, the authorities still expected people to support the war and used lots of propaganda* to build support.

Those who actively campaigned against the war could find themselves in court. For example, members of an organisation called the Peace Pledge Union*, who posted anti-war posters, were put on trial, but their case was dismissed by the judge.

Changes in social attitudes

During the Second World War, official attitudes to COs were quite different from the First World War. In the Second World War people were being asked to unite against Hitler as a tyrant, and Nazism as a movement that persecuted minorities. In this context, harsh punishments for COs would have been seen as hypocritical.

On the other hand, public opinion could still be hostile towards those who refused to fight, when most people felt they were making great sacrifices for the war. Some COs were verbally abused in public – or even attacked. Others lost their jobs, because their employers disapproved of their actions.

Source E

Joyce Allen was a member of the Peace Pledge Union (PPU). Here she describes what happened after she decided to register at a CO.

"When conscription came in I was teaching. I could have asked for exemption, but I wanted to register as a CO... [Even though the school wanted to sack me they] didn't get rid of me: it was difficult to get staff then. I had over 40 supportive letters – the bulk of them from men in the RAF! I think they were scared out of their wits, these young chaps dropping bombs, and wished they could get out of it. The man who was giving me Latin lessons, though, refused to teach me. A member of the PPU offered to teach me instead, and she put the fee I paid her into the PPU funds."

Activities ?

1. Write down two headers – 'Positive reactions' and 'Negative reactions'. From Source E, identify reactions to Joyce's decision to be a conscientious objector, and note each under the relevant header.

2. Write a list of questions that Joyce could have been asked at the tribunal. They could cover her motives, her views about the war, and other war work that she would be willing to do instead.

3. Discuss with a partner how Joyce might have replied to each question.

Exam-style question, Section B

Explain one way in which treatment of witchcraft in the period 1500–1750 was similar to the treatment of conscientious objection in the 20th century. **4 marks**

Exam tip

For this question you should identify a similarity and add information from both periods to support it. You could show knowledge of the actions of either the authorities or the general public.

Summary

- Some men refused to fight in the war as they said their conscience would not allow it. After 1916 they were viewed as criminals.
- The Military Service Act included a section called 'the conscience clause' which allowed men to refuse conscription on the grounds of conscience. Very few were granted this exemption.
- Prison was the most common punishment for COs who refused war work in the First World War.
- In the Second World War, government attitudes to COs were less harsh, but public opinion was generally still hostile.

Checkpoint

Strengthen

S1 Name three punishments faced by COs in the First World War.

S2 What types of work were COs offered by the authorities in the First World War?

S3 What was the Peace Pledge Union?

Challenge

C1 What was the significance of the 1916 Conscription Law in changing the treatment of those who opposed fighting?

C2 Why did the government imprison absolutists during the First World War?

How confident do you feel about your answers to these questions? Discuss any you are unsure about with a partner then try rewriting your answers together.

During the 1950s, a number of controversial executions meant the public became increasingly critical of capital punishment. One of these was the case of Derek Bentley, a young man found guilty of murder and executed in 1953.

The Bentley case and public opinion

Many people in Britain disagreed with the sentence. On the night of the execution, 5,000 protestors met outside Wandsworth Prison chanting, 'Murder!' There were angry confrontations with police, and protestors ripped down and burned the death notice posted on the prison gates.

Derek Bentley's family used the media to promote their cause, and through songs, films and books his case became widely known. The Bentley family campaigned for over 40 years. Derek Bentley was eventually pardoned* in 1993, and in 1998 the conviction for murder was quashed.

Key term

Pardon*

To let a person off the punishment after they have been convicted of a crime; or, as in this case, an official acknowledgement that the punishment was unjust.

Source A

Derek Bentley's parents, sister and brother, on their way to an appeal hearing in London. The appeal was unsuccessful – and Bentley was hanged in 1953.

Source B

Photograph of PC Sidney Miles who was killed in 1952. Derek Bentley was executed for his murder.

Key term

Joint enterprise*

When an accomplice to a crime is held jointly responsible for the crime.

Extend your knowledge

Other controversial executions

Timothy Evans was executed in 1950 for the murder of his wife and baby. However, it was later discovered that a serial killer was responsible for their deaths.

In 1955, Ruth Ellis was hanged for the murder of her boyfriend. Many people believed Ellis should have been allowed to plead diminished responsibility because her boyfriend was violent and abusive, but this was not allowed for murder trials at the time.

Derek Bentley trial, December 1952

Victim – Sidney Miles, policeman, shot during an attempted burglary

Accused

Christopher Craig
16 years old, fired the gun that killed the policeman.

Derek Bentley
18 years old, there when the murder took place but did not fire the gun, mental age of 10.

Case for prosecution

- Craig fired the gun. Bentley shouted "Let him have it." This makes him jointly responsible for the murder as he encouraged Craig.
- Bentley has a history of criminality – has been in youth detention.
- Bentley has a low level of intelligence but was not insane and was aware of and responsible for his actions.

Case for defence

- "Let him have it" could mean, "Let the policeman have the gun." There are questions about whether he really said it.
- Bentley didn't have a weapon. Handed himself over to police.
- Bentley has a learning disability and a mental age of 10.

Jury

Finds Craig and Bentley guilty, recommends mercy for Bentley.

Judge's sentence

Craig can't be hanged as under 18. Sentenced to long prison term. Bentley is guilty of the murder under joint enterprise law*. Sentenced to death by hanging.

Figure 4.6 Outline of the Derek Bentley case.

Source F

Metropolitan Police H Division report by Superintendent Thomas Arnold, 6 November 1888.

On the morning of 30th Sept. last my attention was called to some writing on the wall [in] Goulston Sreet Whitechapel which consisted of the following words: "The Juwes are the men that will not be blamed for nothing." I knew that in consequence of a suspicion having fallen upon a Jew named 'John Pizer' alias 'Leather Apron' having committed a murder in Hanbury Street a short time previously, a strong feeling existed against the Jews generally. I was apprehensive [worried] that if the writing were left it would cause a riot. An Inspector was present with a sponge for the purpose of removing the writing when the Commissioner arrived on the scene.

Activities ?

1 Study Sources B, D and F. What similarities and differences can you identify between the three sources in discussing attitudes people held towards Jewish immigrants?

2 Study Source E. What do you think is the Superintendent's main concern?

3 Research the activities of Bakunin and the anarchists, and the Irish nationalist Fenians, at the end of the 19th century. Which posed the greatest threat to peace and stability in East London?

Summary

- By the 1880s, there had been two distinct waves of recent immigration into the Whitechapel District: Irish and Eastern European.
- In both cases, there were fears that the immigrants brought with them dangerous political views.
- Immigration seemed to be a threat to local people's options for housing and jobs.
- Immigrant groups were likely to be stereotyped as dangerous criminals.

Checkpoint

Strengthen

S1 Say how Sources B–E each show that public opinion was being manipulated or changed.

S2 Explain the hostility shown to the Irish immigrant community in Whitechapel.

S3 Explain the hostility shown to Eastern European immigrants in Whitechapel.

Challenge

C1 Explain which changes in public opinion from S1 would be particularly challenging to the Met.

C2 Draw up a table for Sources B, C and E with a column for each source. In each column, list three anxieties felt by local people about the immigrant community, supported with quotes from the sources.

How confident do you feel about your answers to these questions? Reread the text and try again. Your teacher can give you some hints.

Evaluating usefulness: COAT method

When considering how useful a source is to a particular enquiry, first:

- **identify** content specifically valuable to that enquiry, rather than just general information
- using that material, look carefully at the **provenance** of the source and consider the author's purpose.

First, think about the content: Is what the content says typical of what others are saying about the topic? Does the author have some reason to give an unbalanced view of his or her content? This will help show how useful the source is.

Consider the following criteria when evaluating the content:

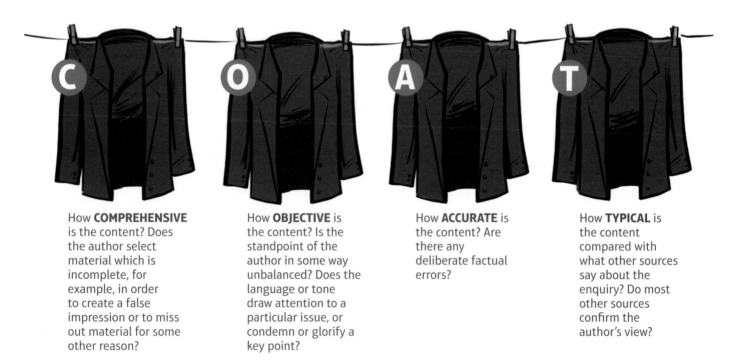

How **COMPREHENSIVE** is the content? Does the author select material which is incomplete, for example, in order to create a false impression or to miss out material for some other reason?

How **OBJECTIVE** is the content? Is the standpoint of the author in some way unbalanced? Does the language or tone draw attention to a particular issue, or condemn or glorify a key point?

How **ACCURATE** is the content? Are there any deliberate factual errors?

How **TYPICAL** is the content compared with what other sources say about the enquiry? Do most other sources confirm the author's view?

Figure 5.6 The COAT method.

In summary, to work out how useful the content of a source is – put on your 'COAT'.

Consider this enquiry: 'How useful are Sources B and C (pages 162–163) for an enquiry into the problems encountered by the people of Whitechapel as a result of widespread immigration during the years 1881–90?'

Beginning with Source B, the material useful for the enquiry is:

1 "The newcomers have gradually replaced the English population in whole districts… "

2 "… they have taken over many streets and lanes and alleys. They fill whole blocks of model dwellings… "

3 "… they have introduced new trades as well as new habits… "

4 "… [they] go their own way independent of the great stream of London life… "

How **comprehensive** is this material? The content focuses on how Jewish people have taken over certain areas (1), including model dwellings (2), and have brought in new forms of employment and lifestyles (3). It also suggests that Jews do not integrate with existing Londoners (4). But Jewish people also brought a new diversity of culture, flourishing trade and a dedicated work ethic, which suggests that the source to some extent gives the wrong impression of the new immigration.

The author has also been selective in focusing on points of criticism, which is not a particularly **objective** approach. The author claims that Jewish people took over large sections of the very housing that had been built to improve the area at the expense of the existing residents – possibly an exaggeration. This might call into doubt the source's **accuracy**.

Nevertheless, there are parts of the source that are not wholly negative – new trades, for example. Does it reflect what other commentators wrote or said? How **typical** is the standpoint taken by the author?

To write a good response about the usefulness of a source's content, you need a working knowledge of the circumstances in which the author was writing. This is called the historical context – the information given in Section 5.3. Bring this to bear to estimate what weight to give a source in helping with the enquiry and use your own knowledge to decide whether the content is exaggerated or accurate.

Finally, remember that to make a full evaluation of the usefulness of a source, you also need to consider its provenance.

Activity	?
With your teacher's guidance, try the COAT approach on Source C (page 163).	

5.4 Police organisation in Whitechapel

H Division

The Metropolitan Police force was split into 20 divisions, each responsible for a district of London and named with a letter of the alphabet. Whitechapel was covered by H Division.

The division was run by a superintendent and a chief inspector, with the support of 27 inspectors and 37 sergeants. The sergeants supervised around 500 ordinary officers, or constables, who went out on the beat.

There were also 15 detectives assigned to H Division from CID.

On patrol – a beat constable's shift

• A typical day (or night) for an H Division beat constable began with him and his colleagues marching out into Whitechapel. When the constable reached his beat – the area he was to patrol – he dropped out of the marching column and started work.

• At night, stopping and questioning people to find out what they were up to was an important part of the policeman's task.

• At certain times, the constable would meet up with his beat sergeant to discuss what had happened so far, and this conversation was written down in his diary.

• If a beat constable was found to be away from his beat, or missed a crime committed on his beat – and could not give a very good reason – he could be fined or dismissed.

• The work was often boring and sometimes dangerous. Pay was not especially good. All these things meant that the quality of recruits was variable. Sergeants would follow constables to ensure they were doing their duty – not sleeping in doorways or idly chatting.

Source A

Extract from *The Times* newspaper in 1853.

The professional policeman, clothed as such, exhibits the strength of a dozen rioters and paralyses opposition by the power that is felt to be at his back, the English law.

Attitudes to H Division

By the mid 19th century, the Metropolitan Police, founded in 1829, were beginning to enjoy a respectable reputation as keepers of the peace and upholders of the law. In many areas, the policeman was seen as a reliable and helpful 'Bobby'. Most ordinary working people wanted respectability and good order in their streets, and while they may not have counted the local policeman as a friend, they did accept that the police were there to help protect that good order.

But in more deprived districts, like Whitechapel, the police were seen in a more negative light and attacks by violent gangs were relatively common (see Source B). The main reason for the unpopularity of the police was the economic depression and widespread poverty of the 1870s–90s. When discontent boiled over into public protests and the police were called in, they were seen as upholders, not of the law, but of unpopular government decisions. In this situation, they soon got a reputation for heavy-handedness and violence – despite the fact that they didn't carry any weapon more lethal than a truncheon.

Source B

A story published in *The Illustrated Police News*, 2 June 1883, about a gang attack on a Whitechapel policeman.

Savage Attack Upon A Policeman

John Harris, Jane Reynolds and Alfred Lindsey were charged in committing a murderous assault on Dennis Mortimer, a constable... Constable Mortimer heard loud cries of 'Stop him!' and as he tackled Harris a mob of young ruffians collected around him and commenced pelting him with stones and hitting him with sticks. Mortimer made strenuous efforts to protect himself, but on drawing his truncheon, according to a witness, the female Reynolds wrenched it from his hand and struck him on the side of the head with it, and another girl also hit him about the head. The prisoner and his gang made their escape, leaving the constable unconscious.

Policing Whitechapel

Whitechapel was a breeding ground for crime – ranging from petty theft to murder. This made H Division's task particularly challenging. Many of the crimes committed were directly linked to the high levels of poverty and unemployment – people with no work would resort to crime rather than starve or go into the workhouse.

Prostitution

It was even harder for women to find work than men and many became prostitutes* in order to survive. While some worked in brothels* or could afford to rent a room,

Key terms

Prostitute*

A person who offers sexual activity in return for payment.

Brothel*

A house where one or more prostitutes work.

others walked the streets where they were vulnerable to assault and rape.

This required sensitive police management to enforce the law. Prostitution was not illegal, but it was seen as a social problem that needed to be monitored.

With no contraception available, abortions were common. They were performed in conditions that meant many women died from infection or surgical shock. Police turned a blind eye to the operations. The Victorian mentality was often that 'unfortunates' (as some middle-class commentators called prostitutes) got what they deserved. There was little understanding that the alternative to prostitution might be starvation.

By 1888, it was estimated that there were 62 brothels in Whitechapel and 1,200 prostitutes – a measure of the hard lives lived by its residents.

Alcohol

For many people living in Whitechapel, the only escape they had from their terrible lives was drink, and they quickly became helpless alcoholics. Very strong drink was affordable for all but the poorest and there pubs and gin houses on every corner. For example, in just one mile (1.5 km) of the Whitechapel Road there were no less than 45 buildings serving as pubs or gin palaces*, as well as a number of opium dens*. Drunkenness often turned to violence, and alcoholics could turn to crime to get the money to buy more drink.

Key terms

Gin palace*

Extravagant, richly decorated gas-lit shop selling gin across a counter. Gin was a cheaply available, potent alcohol, popular with the poor. The light and splendour made a stark contrast with the dark, dirty streets.

Opium den*

A place where the drug opium was sold and smoked. Despite the name, the places could vary in appearance from an elegant bar room to a dark cellar.

Source C

A drawing in the *Illustrated Police News*, published on 2 June 1883. It accompanied the news report shown in Source B.

SAVAGE ATTACK ON A POLICEMAN.

Many immigrants, in common with local people, found themselves without work and living in common lodging houses. Here, tensions between different nationalities could be at their highest and policing most difficult. The rookeries, narrow alleys and courts posed another problem for H Division. The confined spaces, poor lighting and multiple entrances and exits meant there were always corners where criminals could hide.

Protection rackets

Some of the violence in Whitechapel was stirred up by gangs like the Bessarabian Tigers and the Odessians, both made up of immigrants from Eastern Europe. These gangs demanded protection money from small business owners. Anyone who refused to pay would have their shop or market stall smashed to pieces. The gangs also attacked each other. Ordinary people were afraid to report gang members to the police in case the violence turned on them. As a result it was almost impossible to gather enough evidence to arrest gang members or put them on trial.

Because they were overstretched and understaffed, H Division made no attempt to shut down fights and other criminal activities in some areas of Whitechapel, which they would have acted against in other neighbourhoods. One policeman recalled being advised by an old Irishman to keep out of the slum of Ewer Street – if there was a fight, it was sensible to let them get on with it.

Police in the Whitechapel community

Local authorities tended to regard the constable as a kind of social worker. By the 1870s, there were 82 government laws describing what the Metropolitan Police should do when dealing with a wide range of issues, including: vagrancy, lunatics*, pubs, street traffic, sewage and litter, coinage, children, runaway horses, fires and accidents.

Key term

Lunatics*

In Victorian times this term was used to describe people with serious psychological disorders.

One of these laws was the Metropolitan Streets Act of 1867, which introduced further regulations concerning street trading and traffic control, and made the muzzling of dogs compulsory. This law was soon dropped as it was ignored by the public, including the well-off, respectable classes (Source D).

Some of these social work tasks brought the police into immediate conflict with Whitechapel residents.

- When they acted as poor relief officers – conducting people to the workhouse, or children to school – they met great hostility.
- Attempts to control prostitution were resented by women whose very lives depended on earning enough to escape starvation.

On the other hand, the poor people of Whitechapel could see that H Division also provided real benefits: hosting soup kitchens (often to try to get information from witnesses, as the Home Office discouraged offering money); looking after stray children; and stopping runaway horses. Most people felt that a police force was necessary – it was just their methods and priorities that were at fault.

Activities

1. Explain how far Sources C and D agree about the role of the beat constable in East London.

2. What differences do you note between the image (Source C) and the account published alongside it in the 'Illustrated Police News' (Source B)?

3. In groups, discuss the benefits and drawbacks of each of these types of source for the historian.

Source D

A cartoon published in *Fun* magazine, 15 August 1868. *Fun* was a weekly magazine aimed at well-educated readers.

DOG AND DODGE.

Policeman :—"You must put that dog's muzzle on, sir!"

Wide-awake Party :—"Excuse me, Robert, you're mistaken. The order is that no dog shall be allowed in the streets without a muzzle. As you perceive, he has got a muzzle, but prefers carrying it!"

In general, many people felt that the police were rather too concerned with promoting good manners among the residents – at the expense of keeping them safe. Concern for crime prevention led police to be seen as interfering busybodies who were imposing what they believed to be 'civilised' behaviour. This role could be unpopular with residents, who thought their police should act less like teachers and more like criminal catchers.

Overall, poor people needed the police to defend them, and because they were figures of authority, they were able to do this. However, the fact that policemen were in authority was also the reason they were resented, as people did not like being told what to do in their everyday lives.

Activity ?

In groups, prepare to debate how far Sources A–D support this statement from the magazine *The Edinburgh Review*: 'In East London the police should be praised for their handling of public order and for an improvement in public peacefulness and decency'. The article was written in 1852, many years before the period we are looking at. Do you think the author would have taken the same view if he had been writing in 1888?

Summary

- Police were often seen as the government in uniform, representing unpopular laws. This made them unpopular and there were many physical attacks on them.
- Prostitution, alcoholism and the physical layout of the narrow streets gave the police particular challenges.
- Police numbers were too few to cope with lawlessness, so some rougher areas were left without police supervision.
- Many people believed the police were too concerned with enforcing irrelevant regulations at the expense of preventing serious crime.

Checkpoint

Strengthen

S1 Describe in detail the different kinds of opposition – suggested in Sources C and D – that the Metropolitan Police faced when they carried out their duties.

S2 Give examples to show that police could not always cope with lawlessness in the East End of London in the late 19th century.

Challenge

C1 Explain which of the different types of opposition you described in S1 would be the most difficult for the Metropolitan Police to overcome. Give reasons for your answer.

C2 Use evidence from the sources to justify the statement in the summary above that residents resented the police's interference on minor issues.

How confident do you feel about your answers to these questions? If you are unsure, go back to the text and reread the sources to find the evidence you need.

5.5 Investigative policing in Whitechapel

Learning outcomes

- Understand the problems posed for H Division by both the media and their rivalry with the City of London police, during the investigation of the Jack the Ripper murders.
- Know about the detective techniques used in the investigation.
- Understand how investigative methods changed as a result of the Ripper case.

The Jack the Ripper murders

In 1888, five women were murdered in and around Whitechapel. The victims were:

- Mary Ann Nichols, found in Buck's Row on 31 August
- Annie Chapman, found in the back yard of 29 Hanbury Street, Spitalfields, on 8 September
- Elizabeth Stride, found in Berners Street on 30 September
- Catherine Eddowes, found in Mitre Square, Aldgate, also on 30 September
- Mary Jane Kelly, found inside 13 Miller's Court, Dorset Street, Spitalfields on 9 November.

The police believed that all had been killed by the same person. The murderer was never caught but has been given the popular nickname 'Jack the Ripper'.

The investigation into the murders provides a case study within which to assess the challenges faced by the police, and methods of investigative policing at this time.

Source A

A drawing from *Famous Crimes Past and Present*, 1903. PC Neil discovers Nichols's body in Buck's Row.

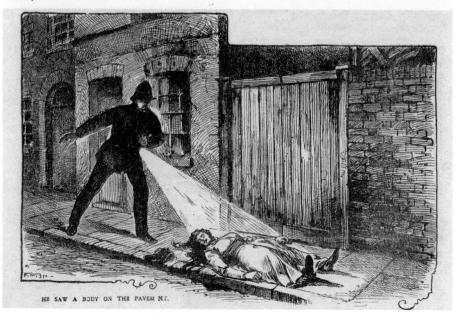

HE SAW A BODY ON THE PAVEMENT.

173

Source B

An inquest sketch of the body of Catherine Eddowes by Frederick William Foster, showing details of extensive mutilation. Sketches were often used to illustrate the methods of violent criminals and to link incidents to previous murders.

Source C

A letter sent on 27 September 1888 to the Central News Agency was at first believed to be a hoax but was later reproduced on this poster, which appeals to the general public for information.

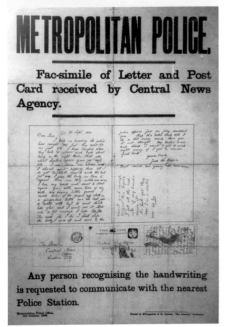

The problem of police and the media

Inspector Frederick Abberline and his CID team were assigned to the Jack the Ripper case by the Metropolitan Police, to assist the uniformed men of H Division. Almost immediately, their task was made much harder by more than 300 letters and postcards sent to them, or to the newspapers, by men claiming to be the murderer.

Source C helps to show the development of police methods in the Ripper inquiry. The police thought this 'Dear Boss' letter important enough to reproduce in newspapers and wall posters, hoping someone would recognise the handwriting.

The problem of police force rivalry

A short time after the discovery of Catherine Eddowes's body, PC Alfred Long of H Division discovered an important clue on Goulston Street – half a mile away. It was a piece of Eddowes's apron, smeared with blood and faeces (human waste). In the alleyway behind, there was a message scrawled in chalk on the wall: 'The Juwes are the men that will not be blamed for nothing'.

174

Summary

- The failure to deal with the Ripper murders in 1888 led to enormous criticism of H Division, the Metropolitan Police and the CID team at Scotland Yard.
- Police methods were inadequate, but criticism was often unfair and paid no attention to the severe obstacles faced in carrying out an effective investigation.
- Some lines of inquiry by the CID in 1888 were imaginative and resourceful, given their lack of scientific knowledge compared with modern day police forces.
- The Metropolitan Police were slow to learn the lessons of the failed Ripper investigation, and improvements in detection were modest up to 1900.
- There were considerable improvements in lighting, housing and health – all as a direct result of national concern about the East End serial killings.

Checkpoint

Strengthen

S1 For Sources B–E, list one way in which each source shows that police were making logical choices in their investigation of the Ripper case.

S2 Explain why the Vigilance Committee was such an obstruction to policing.

S3 Suggest three ways in which the Ripper murders led to better living conditions in Whitechapel.

Challenge

C1 Look at the difficulties the police faced in their Ripper enquiries. Which of these obstacles do you think was the most damaging to the police investigation? Explain your answer.

C2 How far do you agree that changes in the environment of the Whitechapel district were the most important outcome of the Jack the Ripper investigation?

How confident do you feel about your answers to these questions? If you are unsure, form a group with other students, discuss the answers and then record your conclusions. Your teacher can give you some hints.

Asking questions: Whitechapel workhouse

Historians ask themselves three sorts of questions: about content, provenance and context. Look at Source A.

Source A

A sketch showing residents of the Whitechapel workhouse at Christmas 1874.

CHRISTMAS IN THE WHITECHAPEL WORKHOUSE.

Content questions: What are you looking at? You have some important help from the caption, but even without that, you can see Source A shows the residents of some kind of communal residence at Christmas.

Provenance questions: Now you need the caption! Remember, for provenance, you need to break things down into nature, origin, and purpose.

- Nature – it's an artist's sketch.
- Origin comes from the caption – this was drawn, possibly at the Whitechapel workhouse, and possibly from memory, during the festive season in 1874.
- Purpose can be hard for a drawing such as this. Does it look like it was set up specially? Might it be for use as propaganda? In this case, it is fairly easy to think of a propaganda purpose. Perhaps it was drawn to record the excellence of charity provision to the poor by Londoners.

Context questions: You know several things that are relevant to Source A, including the following:

- The idea of the workhouse was that conditions should be worse than those that could be provided by a labourer for his family.
- Among residents of workhouses were the old, sick, disabled, orphans and unmarried mothers.
- Because the residents were made to wear a uniform they felt humiliated.

So, if you were asked how useful Source A is, you could say something like this, covering content, provenance and context:

'Source A is useful because it shows the residents of the Whitechapel workhouse being cared for at Christmas. Although we don't know why it was drawn, it is likely to have been for propaganda, because the Poor Law administrators wanted to show the workhouse system in a good light'.

What this does (and what you can do) is explain why the source is useful, using criteria based on the three types of question.

Activities ?

1 In small groups, study Source C (page 185). Answer the three types of question:

   a content questions

   b provenance questions

   c context questions.

2 Compare your answers with others. You probably came up with some different answers. Does this mean one group has to be wrong?

Source B

From the novel *Captain Lobe* by Margaret Harkness, published in 1889. It features the new Whitechapel workhouse at South Grove.

The Whitechapel Union is a model workhouse; that is to say, it is the very purpose of the Poor Law made into stone and brick. The men are not allowed to smoke in it; the young women never taste tea, and the old ones may not have a cup during the long afternoons, only at half-past six o'clock morning and night, when they also receive a small hunch of bread with butter scraped over the surface, which is so dear to their hearts as well as their stomachs. The young people never go out, never see a visitor, and the old ones only get one holiday in the month. Then the aged poor people may be seen skipping like lambs outside the doors of this prison, while they jabber to their friends and relations. A little gruel morning and night, meat twice a week, that is the food of the grown-up people, seasoned with hard work and prison discipline. What shall we say of the woman, or man, hurt by misfortune, who must come there or die in the street? Why should old people be punished for their existence?

Source C

A photograph taken in the women's ward of Whitechapel workhouse infirmary in 1902.

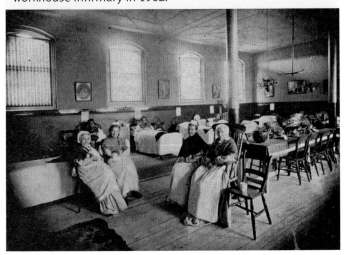

The content of Source B is fairly easy to understand, but the provenance makes it a little more difficult to assess. Although you might think it is factual account

Source D

From a survey of all London's workhouse infirmaries conducted in 1866 by the Poor Law Board. The Board consisted of elected officials who reported on conditions in workhouses in their areas. These comments are about the Whitechapel workhouse.

- Ventilation was inadequate and there was a problem with the drains in the male imbeciles' basement [where people with psychiatric illnesses were housed].
- There were insufficient nursing staff and the medical officers were overworked and underpaid.
- There was very little furniture in the sick wards other than the beds.
- The beds were inadequate in several respects.
- Only three roller towels a week were provided for a large ward, together with a pound of soap which was also used to wash the furniture. A single comb per ward was provided.
- The general sick had no games although dominoes were provided for the imbeciles.
- A separate ward for sick children should be provided.
- The labour ward should be moved so that screams could not be heard in adjacent wards.

of life in the workhouse, it is written in a novel, and is therefore fictional. It is likely to be based on the author's experiences of the area, but we cannot be sure it represents the true nature of South Grove workhouse.

Source C, on the other hand, is a photograph, preserving a moment in time from the past. We don't know all we might like to about the origin, but – since it is taken in the workhouse and its purpose is probably to show that conditions there are very good for sick people – this helps us to gain an understanding of workhouse life. We must be cautious, however, as such photographs are almost always posed to show life at its best.

One thing Source C does not tell you is how many people were resident in the infirmary. There is a reason for this. Those who were in charge of workhouses such as South Grove, knew only too well that living conditions were overcrowded, and may be the subject of the kind of criticisms featured in Source D.

Source D is a good example of the way a source prompts the historian to ask new questions and look for new sources. Source D raises a question because of its detailed criticism, which the fictional account in Source B hints at, but which is completely ignored by Sources A and C. What were conditions really like? So the historian looks for another source: for example, records about workhouses at the National Archive. This adds detail: the age, gender and health of residents of the Whitechapel workhouse at this time, including lots of letters written by those who were in charge. This prompts another question: was this a typical Victorian workhouse? So the historian then compares the record for Whitechapel with that of other workhouses run by Poor Law administrators.

Asking questions in the exam

The exam gives you a start by asking questions. The best way to do well is to ask some more questions – to establish the criteria you will use to make and explain your judgements, and to help you work out the best answers. The criteria you use as the reasons for your answer are one of the main things you will get marks for. So:

- ask yourself the questions
- use the questions to help you decide the best criteria
- use the criteria to explain your answer.

Activities ?

1   In small groups, consider one bullet point of Source D each. Search online for the 1866 report on workhouses.

   a   Make notes on the details mentioned in your bullet point. Are these typical weaknesses or criticisms of all workhouses – or of Whitechapel in particular?

   b   Which of the things you discovered would you expect to find reported in a national newspaper?

2   Now look at Source E. It was drawn for inclusion in a local newspaper. How does this add to your understanding of the value of local newspapers?

3   Compare your answers with those of the other groups, then discuss these two questions:

   a   How useful is Source E for studying the lives of the poor children of Whitechapel?

   b   Are local newspapers a special type of source that tell you things other sources do not?

THINKING HISTORICALLY   **Evidence (3a)**

The value of evidence

Look at Source B, then work through the tasks that follow.

1   Write down at least two ways in which the account is useful for explaining what conditions were like at South Grove.

2   Compare your answers with a partner, then try to come up with at least one limitation of the source for explaining what conditions were like at South Grove.

3   With your partner, decide how useful this source is for explaining the experiences of all residents at South Grove on a scale of 1 to 10 (10 being very useful).

4   What if the source was used to answer the question: 'How were young people cared for at South Grove?'

   a   Write down any ways in which the source is useful for answering this new question.

   b   Write down any limitations for answering the new question.

   c   Can you think of another enquiry about the South Grove workhouse for which this would be a useful source? Write it down and score the source on a scale of 1 to 10.

5   Compare your scores out of 10. How does the question being asked affect how useful a source is? Explain your answer.

6   Can you think of any other factors that might affect the usefulness of the source?

Local newspapers

Source E shows you some of the strengths and weaknesses of local newspapers as sources. The illustration shows a child escaping from the St Giles workhouse, not far from South Grove. Most national newspapers would focus on workhouse conditions in general; but, in a local newspaper, just about everybody who read it must have known that particular workhouse. A local newspaper shows the effects of unusual stories in a single area, and gives us insights into normal life. This account would certainly back up the experiences written in Margaret Harkness's novel (Source B), but might not be typical of workhouses as a whole.

Source E

A sketch from the *Illustrated Police News* (1882). It shows a boy escaping from a local workhouse.

Using the range of sources

In the examination, you are asked to suggest a possible question and a type of source that you could use to follow up another source. As an example, this is what you might do if asked this about Source D. The framework of the question helps you through the four-stage process.

a The detail you might follow up could be one of the problems listed, e.g. shortage of nursing staff.

b The question you might ask is: 'How common was this type of problem?'

c There are lots of different types of source in this unit. You could suggest any one of these:

  • Evidence presented to parliament committees.

  • Local newspapers.

  • Official regulatory records.

d Lastly, you have to explain the reason for your choice:

  • Parliamentary committee reports (because, if it was common, politicians and experts would probably write down the evidence before suggesting new laws to regulate workhouses).

  • Local newspapers (because, if this survey was reported in a Whitechapel newspaper, such cases would probably always be written about, so you would see if there were other reports elsewhere).

  • Official regulatory records (because Poor Law boards will have records, including lists of all the problems and suggestions for remedies).

Activities ?

Using the range of sources

1 On page 146 you started an exercise summarising the usefulness of different types of sources. Continue this for Sources A to E in this section.

2 Use your answers to Question 1 to help you select sources for each of the enquiries below. For each enquiry, first list types of source that appear in this chapter, then suggest one that isn't used and explain why that type would be useful.

Here's an example to show you what to do:

Enquiry a): Useful sources – a poster, propaganda drawings, a report on a demonstration, local newspapers (they might show more detail of events on the day). Additional source – a diary of someone who was there.

a Why did the police find it difficult to control public demonstrations?

b What was the nature of housing problems in Whitechapel?

c Why was there so much tension between East Enders and immigrants in the 1880s?

d What was the significance of a single event – such as the letter sent to the Central News Agency on 27 September 1888?

e What problems were faced by policemen on the beat?

f What was the impact on workers of the types of trades found in the Whitechapel district?

Recap: Whitechapel, c1870–c1900: Crime, policing and the inner city

There are three questions in this section of the exam paper. This recap section is structured around the demands of the three questions.

- The **Two features quiz** is designed to help you prepare for the first question, which is a factual recall question. However, this isn't the only time you'll need factual recall in the examination, so making sure you have a clear factual framework for 'Whitechapel, Crime, Policing and the Inner City' is important. When you are answering questions about the sources, you need to use your knowledge of the period and interpret the sources in the context of what was happening at that time.

- The **This source is useful for...** table helps you prepare for the second question in the exam, which gives you two sources and asks you how useful they would be for a particular enquiry.

- The **All about the details** activity helps you think about the types of source and how they can be used for new enquiries.

- Finally, the **Advantages and disadvantages of particular types of evidence** table helps to assess their strengths and weaknesses.

Two features quiz

For each topic below, list as many facts or features as you can. Aim to have at least two features for every topic.

1 Bloody Sunday, 1887
2 Whitechapel's 'rookeries'
3 'Model' dwellings
4 'Sweated' trades
5 'Unfortunates'
6 Workhouses
7 Dr Thomas Barnardo
8 Irish 'navvies'
9 Fenians
10 The Whitechapel Vigilance Committee
11 The work of Charles Booth
12 'Leather Apron'
13 The Illustrated Police News
14 Anarchists
15 The 'Dear Boss' Letter, 1888
16 The 'Double Event', 1888
17 The Bertillon System
18 The Social Democratic Federation
19 'Penny Dreadfuls'
20 Local watch committees

This source is useful for...
Copy and complete the table.

Sources	Enquiry	Historical context	One way the source is useful and one way it is not useful
5.1 A (page 151) and D (page 153)	Did crime rates go down in the late 19th century?	Some historians have suggested that improving police forces led to lower crime rates.	Source A is useful because it shows official government figures that show offences were below average in the late 1870s, but you cannot tell if this is typical of the whole period of the enquiry. Source D describes the difficulties with gathering correct statistics, but it does tell us that the police were careful to compile accurate records.
5.5 K (page 179)		The Metropolitan Police tried some unusual techniques in the Ripper investigation.	

All about the details
Copy and complete the table.

Source	Detail	Question I would ask	Type of source I would use	How this might help answer my question
5.1 F (page 154)	Leading opposition politicians, opposed to the present government, have used these riots to their own advantage by shamefully supporting the mob.	Did opposition politicians support the mob?	Records of debates in parliament.	Parliament would record what opposition MPs were saying.
5.3 D (page 164)				

Advantages and disadvantages of particular types of evidence
Copy and complete the table.

Type of source	Advantages	Disadvantages
Memoirs of policemen		They may give a justification of their own actions. They may not recall events from long ago accurately.
Records of the local court	They are official documents detailing evidence from witnesses for both prosecution and defence.	
H Division police station records		
Home Office statistics		
Newspapers		

Preparing for your GCSE Paper 1 exam

Paper 1 overview

Your Paper 1 is in two sections that examine the Historic Environment and the Thematic Study. Together they count for 30% of your History assessment. The questions on the Historic Environment: Whitechapel, c1870–c1900: crime, policing and the inner city are in Section A and are worth 10% of your History assessment. Allow about a third of the examination time for Section A, making sure you leave enough time for Section B.

History Paper 1	Historic Environment and Thematic Depth Study			Time 1 hour 15 minutes
Section A	Historic Environment	Answer 3 questions	16 marks	25 mins
Section B	Thematic Study	Answer 3 questions	32 marks + 4 SPaG marks	50 mins

Historic Environment: Whitechapel, c1870–c1900: crime, policing and the inner city

You will answer Question 1 and Question 2, which is in two parts.

Q1 Describe two features of... (4 marks)

You are given a few lines to write about each feature. Allow five minutes to write your answer. It is only worth four marks, so keep the answer brief and try not to add more information on extra lines.

Q2(a) How useful are Sources A and B... (8 marks)

You are given two sources to evaluate. They are in a separate sources booklet, so you can keep them in front of you while you write your answer. Allow 15 minutes for this question, to give yourself time to study both sources carefully. Make sure your answer refers to both sources.

It should **analyse** the sources:

- What useful information do they give? Only choose points that are directly relevant to the enquiry in the question.
- What can you infer? Work out what evidence they can provide that is not actually **stated** in the source.

You must also **evaluate** the sources.

- Use contextual knowledge – for example, to evaluate accuracy or completeness.
- Use the provenance (nature, origin, purpose) of each source to evaluate the strength of the evidence.
- Make **judgments** about the usefulness of each source, giving clear reasons. These should be based on the importance of the content of the sources, and should also take account of the provenance.

Analyse
Information points
Inferences

+

Evaluate
Using knowledge
Using provenance

Q2(b) How could you follow up Source B to find out more about...? (4 marks)

You are given a table to complete when you answer this question. It has four parts to it:

- the detail you would follow up
- the question you would ask
- the type of source you could use to find the information
- your explanation of how this information would help answer the question.

Allow five minutes to write your answer. You should keep your answer brief and not try to fill extra lines. The question is only worth four marks. Plan your answer so that all the parts link. Your answer will not be strong if you choose a detail to follow up, but then cannot think of a question or type of source that would help you follow it up.

Paper 1, Question 1

Describe **two** features of 'model' dwellings in the Whitechapel district in the late 19th century.

(4 marks)

Average answer

Feature 1:
Model dwellings were new houses designed in the 1870s.

Feature 2:
Model dwellings were the first slum clearance programme in the Whitechapel district.

The answer has identified two features, but with no supporting information.

Verdict

This is an average answer because two valid features are given, but there is no supporting information.
Use the feedback to re-write this answer, making as many improvements as you can.

Strong answer

Feature 1:
Model dwellings were new housing developments designed in the 1870s. The Peabody Estate consisted of new blocks containing nearly 300 flats.

Feature 2:
The Whitechapel Estate model dwellings were an example of the first slum clearance programme, encouraged by the Artisans Dwelling Act. The Estate was built where previously narrow courtyards filled with cramped and unhealthy houses had stood.

The answer has identified two features and describes them in more detail. The origin of the Estate is described very clearly. There is a description of what problems the new houses overcame.

Verdict

This is a strong answer because it gives two clear features of 'Model' dwellings and gives extra detail to make the descriptions more precise.

Sources for use with Section A

Source A

From a report in the *East London Advertiser* newspaper, published 15 September 1888. The writer is commenting on Metropolitan Police Commissioner, Sir Charles Warren's decision to bring in soldiers to help police Whitechapel.

The double stupidity of weakening his detective force and strengthening his ordinary police force from reserves and the military destroys two safeguards of a community. It deprives it of a specially trained force of men with brainpower specially adapted for detective work and it takes away the old community constable, to be replaced by a man with a few years' military service, but with no other qualification for serving the public. Nothing has indeed been more characteristic of the hunt for the Whitechapel murderer than the lack of local knowledge displayed by the police. They seem to know little of the dark alleyways of the neighbourhood and still less of the bad characters who swarm through them.

Source B

A sketch for the *East London Observer*, 13 October 1888, on the training of bloodhounds.

243—Oct. 20, 1888—THE PENNY ILLUSTRATED PAPER—249

SIR CHARLES WARREN'S NEW CRIMINAL TRACKERS: MR. BROUGH'S BLOODHOUNDS BEING TRAINED.

Paper 1, Question 2a

Study Sources A and B in the Sources Booklet (see page 192).

How useful are Sources A and B for an enquiry into the methods used in the police hunt for the Whitechapel murderer in 1888?

Explain your answer, using Sources A and B and your own knowledge of the historical context. **(8 marks)**

Exam tip

Consider the strengths and weaknesses of the evidence. Your evaluation must link to the enquiry and use contextual knowledge. Your reasons (criteria) for judgment should be clear. Include points about:

- What information is relevant and what can you infer from the source?
- How does the provenance (nature, origin, purpose) of each source affect its usefulness?

Average answer

Source A is useful because the 'East London Advertiser' tells us that Sir Charles Warren was stupid, because he took away from the murder inquiry the police with the best brainpower to solve it.

Source A is also useful because Warren was the Metropolitan Police Commissioner, although it is also not useful because this was from a local newspaper that wanted to sell lots of copies when unusual events were going on. The author is describing a couple of things that were wrong with the inquiry. Other methods of trying to catch Jack the Ripper also went wrong, like washing evidence away off a wall.

Source B is useful because the sketch shows that the police were using new ideas such as tracker dogs to try to hunt down Jack the Ripper. It is reliable because we know that Sir Charles Warren ordered an experiment to see if bloodhounds could follow a scent. The sketch shows police leading the dogs through Whitechapel, but the experiments never went further than public parks, so this makes it less useful.

Some useful information is taken from the source. The answer suggests an inference –'best brainpower to solve it', but does not really explain or develop this.

Comments are made about the nature of the source, but they assume that a general need by newspapers to sell copies makes this unreliable. Additional knowledge shows an awareness of other failures of the police operation, but is rather undeveloped.

Comments show that there is information that can be taken from the sketch. Knowledge is added to show that the sketch is reliable. It begins to make an inference ('using new ideas…'). It would be stronger with more developed evaluation.

Verdict

This is an average answer because:

- it has taken relevant information from both sources and shown some analysis by beginning to make an inference (so it is not a weak answer)
- it has added in some relevant contextual knowledge and used it for some evaluation of both the sources – but this is not sufficiently developed
- it does not explain criteria for judgment clearly enough to be a strong answer. The evaluation using the provenance of the sources should be more developed.

Use the feedback to re-write this answer, making as many improvements as you can.

Paper 1, Question 2a

Study Sources A and B in the Sources Booklet (see page 192).

How useful are Sources A and B for an enquiry into the methods used in the police hunt for the Whitechapel murderer in 1888?

Explain your answer, using Sources A and B and your own knowledge of the historical context. **(8 marks)**

Exam tip

Consider the strengths and weaknesses of the evidence. Your evaluation must link to the enquiry and use contextual knowledge. Your reasons (criteria) for judgment should be clear. Include points about:

- What information is relevant and what can you infer from the source?
- How does the provenance (nature, origin, purpose) of each source affect its usefulness?

Strong answer

Source A is an account by the 'East London Advertiser', written during the Whitechapel murders in 1888. We can see that the writer has identified particular weaknesses in the police inquiry, such as pulling out detectives ('with brainpower') and replacing useful local police with random army types ('with no other qualification'). Newspapers were often critical of the inquiry and deliberately obstructed the police with fake letters, etc. However, this account is thoughtful and untypical of the unfair criticisms of journals known as 'Penny Dreadfuls'. It is accurate because Warren did take the steps described. But many sensible things had been introduced into the inquiry, including visits to several pawnbrokers' shops to try to track down missing rings from a victim. Owing to the murderer's savagery, police also visited several lunatic asylums. So Source A is a bit one-sided, ignoring good police work.

> Good analysis of the source linked to relevant knowledge. Own knowledge is used to support the comments on the provenance of this source. It is compared with other similar sources.

Source B is useful because it shows a method of investigating the Whitechapel murders. Dated 13 October 1888, it is a reaction to the increasing desperation shown by the police to catch the Ripper. The portrayal is somewhat accurate because Warren ordered an experiment with bloodhounds in Hyde Park, but is unreliable because these tests never got beyond public parks and this sketch shows Whitechapel streets. As a local newspaper known for exaggeration, it is probably making gentle fun of the new police method. Because of this limited purpose, it does not say anything about logical police methods, but does show clearly one reason why the police were criticised.

> Strengths and limitations of the source are shown and contextual knowledge is used in the evaluation, which also comments on the nature of the source, using details and inferences ('they might succeed'), taking examples from both the sketch and its caption.

Verdict

This is a strong answer because:
- it has analysed both sources, making inferences from them
- it has used contextual knowledge in the evaluation of both sources
- the evaluation takes provenance into account and explains criteria clearly when making judgements.

Paper 1, Question 2b

Study Source A (see page 192).

How could you follow up Source A to find out more about the methods used in the police hunt for the Whitechapel murderer in 1888?

In your answer, you must give the question you would ask and the type of source you could use.

Complete the table below. **(4 marks)**

(see page 192)

Exam tip

Make sure your detail to follow up, your question and your suggested type of source all link and that you explain how the source could help answer the question.

Average answer

Detail in Source A that I would follow up:

The local police were replaced by men with a few years' military service but no local experience.

Question I would ask:

How many local police officers were involved in the hunt for the Ripper?

The question is linked to the detail to be followed up.

What type of source I could use:

Police station records.

How this might help answer my question:

They would include reports from beat officers.

The choice of source is unspecific and the explanation does not show how the source would help answer the question.

Verdict

This is an average answer because the explanation of the choice of source is not developed.
Use the feedback to re-write this answer, making as many improvements as you can.

Paper 1, Question 2b

Study Source A (see page 192).

How could you follow up Source A to find out more about the methods used in the police hunt for the Whitechapel murderer in 1888?

In your answer, you must give the question you would ask and the type of source you could use.

Complete the table below. **(4 marks)**

(see page 192)

Exam tip

Make sure your detail to follow up, your question and your suggested type of source all link and that you explain how the source could help answer the question.

Strong answer

Detail in Source A that I would follow up:

The local police were replaced by men with a few years' military service, but with no local experience.

Question I would ask:

What proportion of the men assigned to the Ripper investigation had strong knowledge of the local community?

The type of source I could use:

Metropolitan Police records stored by Scotland Yard, showing the reports of, and beats patrolled by, H division officers, and the service history of the officers.

How might this help answer my question:

If most of the reports of daily activity, particularly beat reports, were from long-serving men in H Division this would show that the investigation was being carried out by men with local knowledge, but if many reports were from men recently recruited from the army, it would show up the weakness suggested in Source A.

The answer has given a question linked directly to the issue identified.

The explanation is linked back to the question for follow-up and the type of source chosen.

Verdict

This is a strong answer because connections between the source details, the question and the source chosen for follow-up are securely linked.

Answers to recap questions

Chapter 1

1 Nobles, freemen, serfs
2 Tithingmen
3 Two of: trial by boiling water, trial by hot iron, trial by cold water
4 Poaching
5 One of: blinding, castration, mutilation, hanging
6 Somebody who has run away to avoid being arrested or tried. There was no punishment for killing an outlaw.
7 Statute of Labourers
8 Treason
9 The Pope
10 A passage from the Bible. People who wanted a trial in a Church court had to read it to prove they were literate, but it was short and easy to remember so some criminals memorised it.

Chapter 2

1 The criminal was hanged, taken down before they were dead, their stomach opened and, finally, the body was cut into four parts.
2 Make the treatment of vagrants more consistent from parish to parish
3 Patrol the street at night to catch criminals in the act
4 Bridewell
5 Pillory, stocks
6 283
7 *Demonologie*
8 North America
9 1605
10 Witchfinder General

Chapter 3

1 Administering an illegal oath.
2 1778
3 *The State of Prisons in England and Wales*
4 Newgate
5 A punishment in which prisoners walked on a revolving wheel.
6 1856
7 Henry Fielding
8 Home secretary
9 London
10 Two of: Dick Turpin, Jack Shepherd, Black Harry

Chapter 4

1 Speeding, drink-driving
2 Verbal or physical abuse of somebody because of their race, gender, sexuality, or disability
3 1991
4 Police Community Support Officer
5 Young offenders
6 Tribunals
7 1993
8 Age at which someone can be prosecuted and punished for committing a crime
9 Limiting access to buildings and digital devices, for example, using body feature recognition
10 New Hall, Wakefield

Chapter 5

Activity 3, page 153: The sketch is from the *Illustrated Police News*, a 'penny dreaduful'.

Index

Index

for permission to reproduce copyright material:

adapted from Tudor Heretics: Number of people executed for heresy in England and Wales © 1997-2014 ...ucational Publishers Ltd

...xtract on page 22 in Interpretation 1 from Inside The Medieval Mind, episode 2 transcribed, BBC/OU, with permission from the BBC; Extract on page 102 in Interpretation 1 from Sir Robert Peel: the life and legacy by Gaunt, Richard A. Reproduced with permission. Distributed in the US and Canada exclusively by Palgrave Macmillan in the format Book via Copyright Clearance Center; Extract on page 102 in Interpretation 2 from Victorian England: portrait of an age, OUP (Young, GM 1936) p.44, by permission of Oxford University Press, USA; Article on page 111 in Source C from MI5 trailed 7/7 bombers for a year, The Telegraph, 01/05/2007 (Philip Johnston, Duncan Gardham and Richard Edwards), Telegraph Media Group Ltd 2007; Quote on page 117 in Source F from Mr Bill Pitt Croydon North West 7:33 pm, 28th February 1983 HC Deb 28 February 1983 vol 38 cc23-107. Contains Parliamentary information licensed under the Open Parliament Licence v3.0; Extract in Source G on page 118 from Metropolitan Police Annual Report 1986: Sir Kenneth Newman. Contains public sector information licensed under the Open Government Licence v3.0; Extract in Interpretation 1 on page 122 from 'Swinging Sixties: The Abolition of Capital Punishment', History Today 58, Issue 12, with permission; Article on page 123 in Source C from Prisonomics © Vicky Pryce 2013 reproduced by permission of Biteback Publishing; Extract on page 128 in Source C from Diary of Jack Foister, Liddle Collection (Foister, J 1916) Leeds University Library; Extract on page 129 in Source E from Joyce Allen's Story, Peace Pledge Union www.ppu.org.uk with permission; Extract on page 148 in Source E from Henry Hamilton Fyfe recalls the events of 'Bloody Sunday' The Times archive, 14 Nov 1887; Extract on page 152 in Interpretation 1 from Crime and Criminals of Victorian London, Phillimore & Co Ltd (Gray, A) p.55, with permission from The History Press; Barnado's Motto on page 160 with permission from Barnardos; Article on page 168 in Source A from The Times, 7th Dec 1853.

Picture credits

The publisher would like to thank the following for their kind permission to reproduce their photographs:

(Key: b-bottom; c-centre; l-left; r-right; t-top)

Alamy Images: Chronicle 93, 128, Classic Image 59, Granger, NYC 42, John Frost Newspapers 175, Mary Evans Picture Library 173, Paul Doyle 109, Pictorial Press 163, Trinity Mirror / Mirrorpix 110; **Bridgeman Art Library Ltd:** A beggar is tied and whipped through the streets, c.1567 (woodcut) (b/w photo), English School, (16th century) / Private Collection 47, A line of chained convicts from Newgate Prison, Old Bailey, being taken to Blackfriars for transportation, c.1760 (engraving), English School, (18th century) / London Metropolitan Archives, City of London 45, 55, Cott Claud B IV f.59 Pharaoh with his servants: he hangs his chief baker; from the Aelfric Pentateuch, from St. Augustine's, Canterbury, 1025-50 (vellum), Anglo-Saxon, (11th century) / British Library, London, UK / © British Library Board. All Rights Reserved 25, Jack the Ripper: Details of the Whitechapel Murders (engraving), English School, (19th century) / Private Collection / © Look and Learn / Peter Jackson Collection 153, Police Notice to the Occupier Relating to Murders in Whitechapel, 30th September 1888 (print), English School, (19th century) / Private Collection 179l, Sir Charles Warren's new criminal trackers: Mr Brough's bloodhounds being trained (engraving), English School, (19th century) / Private Collection / © Look and Learn / Peter Jackson Collection 179r, Skeletons, Walkington Wold Burials 17; **Getty Images:** Evening Standard / Stringer 122, Hulton Archive 146, Keystone-France 106, 114, Mike Moore 124, Olaf Protze 21, 33, Past Pix 129, Paul Popper / Popperfoto 131, Popperfoto 132, Universal History Archive / Contributor 8, 35, UniversalImagesGroup 62; **Herzog August Bibliothek Wolfenbuttel:** 10; **John Frost Historical Newspapers:** 121; **Mary Evans Picture Library:** 57, 77, 83, 94l, 94r, 184, Grosvenor Prints 72, 89, Illustrated London News Ltd 161, Interfoto / Sammlung Rauch 24, 177, Peter Higginbotham Collection 158, 185, Photo Researchers 181, The National Archives, London, England 85; **National Archives:** 60l, 60r, 100, 151, 157; **Rex Shutterstock:** Alex Segre / Shutterstock 117, Cultura / Shutterstock 115tl, London News Pictures / Shutterstock 9, 116, Shutterstock 115br; **© The British Library Board:** 143, 187, Caledonian Mercury Newspaper, 29 March 1834 76, Fun magazine 1868 171, The British Newspaper Archive (www.britishnewspaperarchive.co.uk) 170; **TopFoto:** 64, 81, 127, British Library Board 157, 162, Topham Picturepoint 174tr, 174bl, World History Archive 23; **University of Maryland:** Morris, William, 1834-1896-https://aeon.lib.umd.edu/nonshib/aeon.dll- Special Collections and University Archives, University of Maryland Libraries 144; **Used with kind permission from Barnardo's www.barnardos.org.uk:** "Dr.Barnardo with children" supplied by Barnardo's 160.

Cover images: *Front:* **akg-images Ltd:** Archie Miles

All other images © Pearson Education

Picture Research by: Jane Smith